WHEN IT CLICKS
THE GUIDE TO MASTERING ONLINE DATING

Harris O'Malley

Other Books By Harris O'Malley

New Game + : A Geek's Guide to Love, Sex and Dating
Simplified Dating: The Ultimate Guide To Getting Better at Dating… Quickly!

Copyright © 2015 Harris O'Malley

All rights reserved
No part of this book may be reproduced in any form or by any electronic or mechanical means, including information storage and retrieval systems, without written permission from the author, except for the use of brief quotations in a book review.
Cover illustrated by Carla Speed McNeil and Jenn Manley
ISBN:978-0-9963772-3-2

To the Paging Dr. NerdLove readers: I can't do it without you guys. And to the WEFugees, the V-Hives and the Sk8Jesuits. We run Bartertown!

Contents

Foreword 9
1. Choosing Your Dating Site 13
2. The Secret to Online Dating Success 25
3. How To Look Good In Photos 44
4. Building The Perfect Profile 64
5. Making Contact 86
6. Taking It Offline 106
7. Get Out of The Offline Dating Mindset 116
8. Why Women Don't Respond 136
9. Learning To Moneyball OkCupid 155
10. Frequently Asked Questions 172
11. The Most Important Advice I Can Offer ... 196
About The Author 200

FOREWORD

I love online dating.

No lie. Online dating is, in many ways, an answer to so many of the problems that people have when it comes to meeting new and amazing potential partners. You're able to set your parameters as wide or as narrow as you want. Want to make sure you're dating someone with the same religious background? You can filter out everyone who doesn't meet that particular criteria. Looking for that 6' tall, blonde PhD candidate/opera singer of your dreams? Dial it in, man and see who's out there.

Moreover, it's *the* most relaxed, low-stress way of meeting incredible women. If you're an introvert, then you don't have to go to loud, crowded bars and scream to be heard. You're able to approach, meet and flirt with women from the comfort and security of your own home. If you get anxious approaching strangers in person, then online dating allows you to relax and take things at your own pace. You have all the time in the world to figure out what you want to say and how you want to say it, instead of getting tongue-tied trying to think about what to say.

You can fit it into your schedule, whether you're a morning person or a night-owl; you can *literally* meet women in your pajamas at any time of day. You can't *do* that in person.

Well, without getting some weird looks, anyway.

(And how she managed to get into your pajamas in the first place, I'll never know.)

But as fun and easy as online dating can be, it can *still* be incredibly frustrating and confusing. Many, *many* people have put up their profile and sent out those pokes, winks and messages only to get thunderous silence in return. They swipe right but never get anyone who matches with them. Women who seem interested will disappear without warning, while others simply flake out every time you try to make a date with them.

But that's where *I* come in. This guide is designed to show you the ropes and teach you how to make meeting women through online dating simple, easy and *fun*. Whether you're looking for a casual hook-up, a friend with benefits situation or the love of your life, this is the instruction manual you've been looking for all this time. I'll walk you through the keys to creating the dating profile that gets attention and how to make sure that the right women - the women *you* want to meet - stop and check you out. You'll learn the secret to dating profile photos that catch people's eyes and show you off to the best effect. You'll learn how to craft the perfect introductory message that will stand out from all the spammy, repulsive messages that frustrate women; yours will stand out from the churn and invite women to write back. I'll help you avoid the most common mistakes that men make when it comes to online dating and understand the reasons why women aren't responding. You'll learn the warning signs of fakes and flakes and be able to avoid them *before* you waste your valuable time. And I'll even guide you through taking the conversation from online to in person.

There're no head games, no magic tricks, no Pick-Up Artist inspired bullshit that only serves to annoy women. There's no "gaming the system" or trickery here. You're going to be learning how to use dating sites *correctly*, in the most intelligent, efficient and optimized manner. You won't be putting up a false front or pretending to be something you're not. This isn't snake-oil, this is about learning how to put your best, most attractive, most *authentic* self forward and finding the people who are right for *you*.

Whether you're looking for a casual hook-up on Tinder or the long-term relationship of your dreams on OKCupid, Plenty of Fish or other sites, this book is going to help you navigate the world of online dating and find the match you're looking for.

ONE

Choosing Your Dating Site

Which Dating Site Is Right For You?

The first - and seemingly most obvious - step when it comes to getting started in online dating is to pick which dating site or sites you are going to use. This is actually fairly significant; if you want to make online dating as efficient and trouble-free as possible, you don't want to spread your presence and attention too thin. The more profiles you have to monitor and maintain, the more time you're going to spend performing that maintenance. It doesn't seem like much of an investment - a little time on one site, a little more on another - but it adds up quickly. Worse, it makes it hard to keep track of who's on which site; if you're trying to find that one profile that caught your eye and have to log into three or four different accounts to try to find them again, you're going to get frustrated pretty damn quickly. It's better to keep your focus narrow, with accounts on one or two sites at a time.

Moreover, not all dating sites are created equal. Different sites have different cultures and demographics, which will directly affect who will show up in your searches and how those people will respond to you . Before you invest your time and money, you want to do your due diligence with dating sites.

First and foremost: consider what you're looking for. Certain sites cater more to particular types of relationships. eHarmony, for example, is *specifically* for people looking for long-term relationships; if you're looking to date a number of people casually, you should look elsewhere. It also has a very rigid structure and specific rules for communicating with your matches, which can make things tedious if you're looking to talk to more than one match at a time. OKCupid, on the other hand, is much more free-wheeling; their membership ranges from people simply looking for platonic friends to casual sex partners to relationships. Match is more relationship-based while apps like Tinder and Grindr are intended as hook-up tools.

This isn't to say that you can't find something that isn't necessarily part of the dominant culture - people can and *do* end up in committed relationships with people they met off Tinder, for example - but it's going to be akin to swimming uphill. It's possible, but you're going to be expending a lot more energy doing so.

Secondly: consider *who* you're searching for. Some sites focus on a very specific audience. Christian Mingle and JDate cater to a user base that prefers to date fellow Christians or Jews; this is great if religion and culture is important to you. Other sites are simply less open to certain demographics. eHarmony famously doesn't allow for same-sex pairings, for example, and is surprisingly picky about who it *does* service; many of my friends were told that the site couldn't match them to *anyone*. If you're looking for a less-traditional relationship - non-monogamous or polyamorous, etc. - then you're more likely to find like-minded people on OKCupid than on Match.

Third: make sure you understand what you're signing up for. Most dating sites will allow you to create a profile for free. Some require a monthly subscription that will then give you unlimited communication with other profiles. Others will require that you buy credits. Some make it hard to cancel a recurring subscription and others make it difficult to remove your profile entirely. Ashley Madison - a dating site designed specifically to match up people looking for extramarital affairs - makes it simple enough to leave but makes it difficult to completely remove your profile. If you want to delete your profile, rather than simply hiding it, you have to pay.

Do your research before you commit; your time is valuable and you don't want to waste it on sites that are - wait for it - not a match for you.

Free Sites vs. Pay Sites

Choosing which sites to join brings up the next question: do you want to focus on free sites or sites that require that you pay to message people? Both have pros and cons to consider.

Free Sites:

Pro: Free sites like Plenty of Fish and OKCupid, as well as apps like Tinder don't put any barriers between you and your potential matches. Once you create a profile, you're free to search and message people to your heart's content. As a result, free sites tend to have a much larger userbase than paid sites. Most free sites make their revenue in one of three ways: via advertising, via selling information to marketers and via upselling premium features such as improved search options and read receipts. This means that free sites have a motivation to keep their users around and active, while paid sites do *not*. An active user is one who's getting served ads; serving up an abandoned or zombie profiles is a very good way to end up with an *inactive* user.

Con: Free sites mean more people sign up. The size of the user base can be a blessing and a curse at the same time; while having more users means more potential matches, it *also* means an increase in potential scammers, catfish[1] and general assholes who make things miserable for everyone. Women on free dating sites frequently end up dealing with an exhausting deluge of inappropriate and offensive messages from asshats and creepers, as well as the innumerable "'sup", "Kik/Snapchat/Skype?" and other time-wasters. Some free sites are also more appropriately called "premium"; Tinder has recently implemented in-app purchases with Tinder Plus and restricts all free users to a limited number of swipes per day.

Paid Sites:

Pro: Paid sites encourage people to take dating seriously. Paying a subscription fee - even one that's relatively reasonable - is going to cut down on the number of fakes, flakes and jerks. Some will argue that pay sites have more attractive users; since beauty is very much in the eye of the beholder, your mileage will obviously vary here. More importantly: paying for a dating site means that people are more likely to respond to messages from new people. A 2009 study found that people who paid for a dating site were more likely to respond to and go out with potential matches than ones who *didn't* pay - and the amount of time they would spend with those dates was directly proportional to how much they had paid. This is part of what's known as the "sunk cost" fallacy - when you've invested in something and can't get your investment back, you're much more likely to stick with it, even if you're not happy with it. In practical terms: when you're paying hard-earned cash for membership on a dating site, you're much more likely to take it seriously because otherwise you've wasted your time and money… and we have a psychological aversion to admitting this.

Cons: There's no motivation to actually match you to somebody. Once you've paid your subscription fee, the site's got your money and you've become part of their marketing strategy - your profile is now part of how they attract new subscribers. See, most paid dating sites will let you put up a *profile* for free but require that you buy a subscription in order to actually *message* people. So if you see somebody you like, you're more likely to actually buy a subscription. As a result: there's a vested interest in *not* showing subscribers to other subscribers; you've both already paid and they get nothing more from you. There's no indication whether any particular profile is a subscriber or not, so you may very well be messaging someone who *can't* message you back. Worse: they may not even be on the site any more; just because somebody cancelled their subscription and abandoned their account doesn't mean that their account is *removed*. That cutie who caught your eye and tempted you into paying for a 6 month subscription may well be a zombie account, with nobody behind it.

It's also worth noting: many paid sites, especially "specialty" sites - sites that cater to various subcultures and offer to set up fellow Goths or geeks or Objectivists - are scams. They're a rent-a-kit dating site; a customized front-end that pulls from a centralized database of members. As a result, you may well end up contacting someone on a dating site specifically for gamers who had no idea that their profile was being served up on other sites. *Caveat emptor* indeed.

WHAT ABOUT NON-STANDARD DATING SITES?

This book focuses primarily on traditional online dating sites, since these have larger, more involved user bases who are specifically looking for relationships. However, if you want to try something different, there *are* a number of non-standard dating sites that have cropped up recently. These sites forgo the usual search-and-message practice for more inventive ways of connecting people that focus less on profiles and more on meeting in person. HowAboutWe has users suggest specific dates such as "How about we have a drink and challenge each other to games of Skee-Ball", while allowing you to search for other dates that might intrigue you. Grouper, on the other hand acts as a sort of blind group-date facilitator; you recruit two wingmen and pay around $17 each. The "leader" of the group is shown profiles to approve or disapprove. If there's a mutual match, Grouper arranges and coordinates a group date at a specific bar; the money kicked covers the first round of drinks, plus a tip for the server.

These can be a fun alternative to standard dating sites, especially if you're the sort of person who's better in person than on paper. However, I wouldn't necessarily recommend them as your *primary* focus for online dating. Very few of them are as firmly established as sites like Match or OKCupid and can feel somewhat gimmicky. I would take a wait and see approach before looking at them as anything other than a diversion.

Then there is the question of trying to meet people on websites that aren't explicitly designed for dating, such as social networking sites like Facebook.

As a general rule, I think this is usually a bad idea. Most social networking sites simply aren't designed with meeting strangers in mind. In fact some, such as Facebook, tend to have issues with making your information *too* available to others. Most people use social networking sites to communicate with their friends and family, rather than to pick up dates. Others have problems with people *assuming* that they're dating sites. FetLife, a popular website for the BDSM community was created as "the Facebook for kinky people"; it's designed to provide a network for fellow kinksters, not to help people find a hook-up. This doesn't stop people from *trying*, mind you... but that's not what the site is for. People who signed up for OKCupid are doing so with the express intent of dating; very few people signed up for Facebook for the same purpose. Making cold approaches - approaching people with whom you have no social connection - on

Facebook, Twitter, Instagram or other social networks is *not* something I recommend. Most people are going to be seriously put off by a complete stranger trying to slide into their DMs.

Now that having been said, some sites actually work quite well for meeting people - provided you don't use them explicitly as a *dating* site. Instead, you'd want to use them as a way of expanding your social circle and possibly finding a match that way. Meetup is a popular way for people to meet and make new friends by connecting you with groups and events based on pastimes you enjoy. This makes Meetup a useful tool in augmenting your online dating strategy, rather than replacing it. After all, one of the perks of online dating is finding people who share the same interests that you do; Meetup can help facilitate this by helping find events that you might enjoy where you can meet like-minded people in person.

Which Sites Do I Recommend?

Speaking strictly from my own experiences, I would recommend OKCupid over most dating sites. Its free options are impressively robust, especially in comparison to competitors like Zoosk and Plenty Of Fish, and the subscription benefits are more useful than just "be allowed to message this person". Their profiles go into greater depth than just a "What's your Story" and your statistics, affording you greater opportunity to show off your personality. The questions and tests give you a greater level of granularity in your searches and while the actual value of its compatibility engine is questionable, the match percentage *does* encourage people to pay attention to your profile. It has less of a turnover in users than paid sites like Match and the culture is more open to different kinds of relationships than most dating sites. It also has the cleanest and most useful design, making it easier to navigate and use; you aren't left fumbling through a chain of links trying to find that *one* option you need to change. Of all the dating sites I've used over the years, it's the one where I've met the most interesting women, gone on the most dates and has - in my opinion - the best overall user experience.

If you were going to focus on *one* dating site, I would recommend OKCupid's A-List subscription. If you were going to use more than one, especially a pay or subscription site, then I would still recommend keeping an active OKCupid account. I would *not* recommend making an app like Tinder your primary online dating focus. Despite its ubiquity, it's still more of a diversion than a full-fledged service and its subscription prices (with fees that vary by a user's age) are dodgy. In my experience, it makes for a better supplemental service to your regular dating site rather than a replacement.

But all of this is strictly my opinion. The best dating site is the site that works for *you*. Find the site that's the best match for the type of person and relationship you're looking for.

Now let's get started on supercharging your online dating experience, shall we?

---

[1] Catfish: people who create fake identities on social media and dating sites. More on them later.

Two

The Secret to Online Dating Success

Act Like A Lover, Think Like a Marketer

I want to let you in on a little secret: most people are doing online dating wrong. This is why so many people have a miserable time when they create their profiles. They send out winks and messages and get nothing but silence in return. They see people checking out their profile, only to disappear into the digital ether. Worse, people you *know* are your type aren't visiting your profile at *all*.

These little frustrations add up quickly; after all, who wants to have yet another reminder that you're at home alone on a Friday night when all these other people are out having a wonderful time? Who needs the mockery of an empty mailbox piled on top of that misery? Small wonder so many people delete their profiles and give up on online dating altogether.

The problem, however, is that these people don't understand the secret to online dating. They waste valuable time and mental bandwidth on the people who aren't responding to them and wonder what's wrong. They've put their heart and soul into their profiles to no avail.

And that's their mistake. They're taking the entirely wrong approach to online dating. So I'm about to impart to you the secret to online dating success: you need to quit thinking like a lover. You need to think like a marketer.

I know this sounds crazy. It feels completely antithetical to the idea of finding a relationship; you're looking to make a connection with somebody - whether that connection is for a lifetime or for 30 minutes of squishy noises - not trying to sell them a product. Treating online dating like an exercise in commerce seems soulless at best and completely cynical and manipulative at worst.

Worse, when you bring "marketing" and "internet" together, what's the first thing that comes to mind?

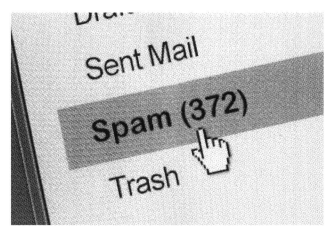

Spammers are the bane of the Internet, the one group that is universally reviled and hated with the passion of a thousand blazing suns. So it's understandable that you might be a little turned off to the idea and wondering what the hell is wrong with me for suggesting it.

Here's the twist though: online dating is *all about the marketing.* Yes you may be looking for your one true soulmate[1]. but dating is, at its core, a numbers game. 99.999% of the population doesn't find somebody on the first try, which is why you want as many people as possible coming to see your profile. Just as importantly, you want to keep those people around long enough to dazzle them with your brilliance (or at least baffle them with your bullshit) and make them decide that yes, they *would* like to get to know you better. This is why marketing becomes important to dating success: you need to be able to snag their attention and hold it. Attention is the currency of online dating – the more you have, the more likely you are to get what you want: dates.

But attention for attention's sake is useless, especially for the purposes of dating. It's incredibly easy to get *shitty* attention. Any woman can tell you: all she has to do is click "Looking for: Casual Sex" in her profile and she will be bombarded with more attention than she knows what to do with[2]. Men, on the other hand, can write something truly disgusting or insulting to women and look forward to being featured on the many Tumblrs devoted to people who make asses out of themselves on OKCupid and enjoy the masses who're only coming by in order to gawk at the train wreck.

What you want is *targeted* attention. You don't want to attract everybody, you want the people whom you're hoping to date. To do *that*, you have to know how they think, what they're looking for and, critically, how to grab them by the eyeballs. You have to understand how to market yourself to them.

Packaging The Product

The first step to thinking like a marketer is to recognize that you need to start with the product (in this case, you) that you're trying to move (i.e. get laid, get dates, what-have-you). As any *Mad Men* fan will tell you, the key to marketing a product isn't the product itself, it's in how you make it appeal to the potential customer. This is why packaging is so important; your product may be great - you're an awesome person that *anyone* would be lucky to date - but if you present it in the wrong way, people are going to be turned off and choose something else. Your profile – your screen name, your photos, your vital statistics and your words – are all part of your packaging and even slight flaws in that packaging can make potential customers (dates) go off in search of products that strike them as more appealing.

In dating, both online and off, first impressions are incredibly important. You only have a few moments to capture somebody's attention and intrigue them into wanting to know more before they move on. If you don't snag those eyeballs right from the jump, you've *already* lost them. This means you need to put your best face forward… literally. The very first thing that people look at, whether they're browsing profiles, swiping left or right, or when they get your message in their inbox is your profile photo. Cold hard truth time: most people are going to let that photo make the difference as to whether or not they're intrigued enough to check you out further. This is *especially* true on Tinder, which is superficial by design. Your profile may be amazing but if you want to snag the attention of the casual browser, you need to have a primary photo that's eye-catching and impressive.

Most online dating sites are designed to let people browse casually, displaying dozens of photos and screen names at a time. It doesn't take very much for this to become a sea of interchangeable selfies, where everybody starts to blur together in a flesh-colored smear. You want yours to stand out from the others in the right way. You want to catch the person's attention and give them just enough information to intrigue them. But it has to be the *right* photo. Our brains are hard-wired to look for faces; that's part of how we make connections with one another. Making it hard to see your face makes it harder to connect with you and makes potential dates more likely to pass your profile by. This means that your primary photo, the one that appears next to your screen-name in your online dating profile, needs to be a well lit shot of your head and shoulders. Not a full body shot - this makes it difficult to see your face. Not something awkwardly cropped from your vacation snaps. Not a moody, arty, Instagram-filtered selfie. Not a picture of you and your bros. Just you. Little things, like a splash of bright color - a colorful shirt, a vibrant colored background - help your photo pop out from the throngs of nearly identical thumbnails. If you *do* use a little strategic color, be sure that the color doesn't cause you to recede into the background; if you make it harder to pick you out, you're negating the point of having the photo in the first place.

Don't worry; we'll cover how to look great in photos in another chapter.

Save your other photos – the ones of you doing cool stuff, hanging out with your friends, and otherwise being awesome – for when they click to your profile; that's part of how you intrigue them further *after* you have their initial attention. Just make sure that you avoid the dating site photo cliches: no posing with "dangerous" animals to make you look brave[3], no showing off the fish you caught[4] and no "check out my abs... ladies" shirtless photos. It's great that you have a six-pack, but deliberately drawing attention to it makes women think of the cast of *The Jersey Shore* – and not in a good way. If you don't have enough imagination to figure out how to get a photo from your time at the beach or waterpark to show that you've got more cuts than Tiesto then you really shouldn't be worried about online dating in the first place.

And for the love of all that's holy, *no selfies in the mirror.* The mirror-selfie is the anti-sex equation.

Once you have the profile photo out of the way, you want to address the other aspects of your dating profile - these are all areas where it is *very* easy to snatch defeat from the jaws of victory. In descending order of importance:

- **Your screen name** – Trust me: people pay more attention to this than you realize. Your choice in screen name says far more than you'd think. A great screen name can inspire a conversation - making a reference to a book or movie you love, a hobby or your career can all lead to someone messaging you to ask questions. A badly chosen screen name, however, is a great way to burn away any goodwill you may have built. Names like "Bushmaster", "GladHeAteHer", "HungLikeAHorse", "Smokedup420" [5] and anything using the number "69," are nature's way of saying "do not touch." There is no amount of irony that can save you from looking like an idiot with these. Also as a personal note: avoid using "88" in your screen name, even if you were born in 1988. Thanks to one date gone horribly wrong, I've discovered that this is frequently Aryan Nation code. Avoid.

- **Your Vital Statistics** – Height, weight, age, hair color, etc. Some people have *very* firm opinions about the range of height, weight and age that they're willing to consider in a potential date. If these don't line up with your photo - and trust me, *many* dudes have tried to get away with saying they had an 'athletic' or 'muscular' build when they clearly didn't - people won't bother sticking around to read your brilliant prose.

- **Your Actual Profile** – 90% of the time, the *last* thing that people check out on your profile. Once you've made it past the initial hurdles, you get to make your pitch. By the time they've gotten to the point of reading your profile, they've *already* confirmed that they're at least a little interested. This doesn't mean you can slack off on your profile mind you. You've got their curiosity. Your profile is how you get their attention.

Practice Good Dating SEO

Another mistake that people mistake when it comes to online dating: they focus too much on being the one who does the searching. It's all well and good to browse those profiles, but you're missing out on half the action. There are women out there looking for *their* perfect match, just the same as you are - in fact, they may very well be looking for someone exactly like *you*. However, all that effort isn't going to do any good if they can't *find* you. You may be their Mr. Right, but if you're not showing up in their searches, then they'll never know and end up moving on to someone else. You don't want that. Too many people just put up a slap-dash profile, cross their finger and hope for the best. Much like with online store-fronts or blogs, you can't just toss your profile out into the great digital sea and hope that somebody stumbles across you by accident. There's entirely too much competition out there to trust that people will find you by random chance. You want to put up those signs and billboards that let the people know: YOU ARE HERE.

In other words: you need to make sure you show up in their searches.

In online marketing, this is known as SEO or Search Engine Optimization: the art of ensuring that you show up more prominently in search engine results[6] than your competition. This concept applies to online dating as much as it does trying to get your blog to the first page of Google search results.

As more and more people sign up for online dating, trying to find someone who matches your standards can be like trying to find a needle in a haystack of nearly identical needles. If you feel like you can't find someone you're interested in, then you're going to cancel your account. Since dating sites are in the business of helping you find the red-haired, board-game loving triathlete of your dreams, they are all about the search parameters. After all: it's in their interest to let you be as specific as possible - the more desirable profiles you find, the more likely you are to stick around. That's why nearly every dating site will allow you to narrow your search by things like height, weight, religion, astrology sign, income, ethnicity, build[7] and - most importantly - *keywords*. Keywords are critical when it comes to raising your visibility and attracting the right attention in online dating sites. People on dating sites are particular about what they're looking for in a potential date, and if you don't let them know that that you have the specific x-factor that they're looking for, they're going to skim right past you like you weren't even there.

This is where the dating SEO comes in.

Part of marketing is getting into the heads of the people you want to have as customers: what are they looking for and how can you provide it? When it comes to dating, you want to think like the people you are hoping to attract: what are they going to be interested in? What qualities are *they* going to be looking for in a potential date – more importantly – how would they *describe* what they're looking for? Is a Doctor Who fan going to look for phrases like "Whovian" or is she more likely to search for "Tardis," "Tennant," or "Smith," or "Donna Noble was the best companion"? Is a sporty, outdoors-y woman going to be looking for "hiking" or "camping"? If she's musically inclined, what kind of music? Would she search for genres (top 40, R&B, jazz) or specific songs or performers ("Uptown Funk," "Anaconda," Nicki Minaj, Drake, Imagine Dragons, etc.)?

Like any good ad man, you're going to want to do some market research; examine the profiles of people *you* would want to date and see how they talk about interests and hobbies. Which phrases seem to come up the most often? Are they general or specific? These phrases are your keywords and you want to make sure that these feature prominently in your profile. Keywords mean that you have to show, not tell; if you're a geek looking for a fellow geek, you don't want to just state "Yup, I'm a nerd." Drop some very specific keywords, whether that you watch *Arrow* and *Game of Thrones* or have a Green Lantern ring. Mention your zombie apocalypse survival plan. If you have a unique feature that others would be interested in, such as tattoos or an interesting hobby, then you want to make sure those figure prominently as well so that potential matches can find it.

Some systems let you tag specific keywords in your profile in order to make them more prominent; others use the Google search API. Even if a particular site doesn't have the option to search by keywords, make sure that the words appear in such a way that they're hard to miss; you want someone skimming your profile to see those keywords and pause long enough to let the *rest* of your profile intrigue them.

MAINTAIN VISIBILITY

Another key to successful marketing is to maintain your visibility in an incredibly crowded market. Popular sites like OKCupid and Plenty of Fish get thousands of new dating profiles every *day*. If you live in a medium to large city, then it's very easy for your profile to disappear in the continual flood of new users. New accounts tend to get the lion's share of attention, often being featured on the site's front page. Fortunately, many sites have ways of highlighting profiles and attracting extra attention. Most dating sites automatically sort search results by recent activity and logins, helping users filter out inactive or zombie dating profiles in favor of people who're more likely to respond.

Other dating sites have different ways of keeping more active members in the forefront. OKCupid, for example, has a column marked "recent activity", which highlights new photos and shows users who have answered questions or edited their profile. Regularly adding new photos to your profile – and rotating out older ones – will help keep your dating profile fresh and attract more attention. In fact, a new primary profile photo can bring back people who've skimmed over you before. It's also a good idea to regularly review and update your profile; not only does the activity raise your profile's visibility, it also helps keep your information relevant. You don't want potential matches judging you on outdated information, after all.

Other sites take things a step further and try to foster a sense of community. Some have blogs and forums where users can talk amongst themselves. Taking part in the community can help bring more attention to your profile as people want to get to know more about you. Of course, if you act like an asshat in the forums, you'll be attracting the *wrong* kind of attention…

A word of caution: several sites have upselling options such as paying to have your profile highlighted or "featured" in other people's searches and inboxes. I have yet to see any evidence that this provides any tangible benefit in terms of receiving messages from potential matches or in responses from people *you* message. In my experience, all this does is tell people that you're willing to pay money to be more visible; not a net positive and possibly a negative in some people's eyes. Personally, I would avoid spending any more money than I absolutely have to on a dating site; the return on investment simply isn't worth the cost.[8]

What Is Your Brand?

Branding is an important part of marketing; it cements the traits and emotions you associate with a particular product. When you think of Apple, you think of clean design, ease of use, and the iPhone. When you think of Tee Fury, you think of amusing shirts and clever pop-culture references. Alcoholic beverage companies want you to associate being classy or being popular or exciting with their drinks, so that you'll buy them in hopes that people will think *you* are classy or exciting.

So what do people think of when they think of you? What traits and emotions are going to be associated with your profile?

Think carefully, because the answer is incredibly important. You don't sell a product by saying "It's OK... I guess," or "Fuck you, you're too stupid to appreciate the glory that is this product," you do it by making the product sound *amazing* and desirable. Many men who use online dating come across as... well, frankly, more than a little bitter and entitled. I can't count the number of men who rant and rave about how unfair dating is and how shallow women are. Any number of Tumblrs feature the many, *many* winning personalities of OKCupid users, highlighting the cranky, the resentful, the desperate, the creepy and the hopelessly self-deluded. It doesn't take very much to screw up an otherwise attractive dating profile. That little comment about not wanting drama or "fake-ass bitches" or how you're a Nice Guy^{TM} and women don't appreciate you is all that it takes to make people decide to give you a hard pass. You want to project an aura of confidence and positivity, not anger or bitterness at being single. Nobody is going to have any compassion for your tales of woe. Complaining about having been wronged before isn't going to get you the sympathy pussy you're hoping for and whinging about how women are hypergamous, game-playing bitches won't help you find the one Cool Girl who's Different

From The Rest. The more you tell women that they're not worth your time (including any variation on "No Fat Chicks" or "$QUALITY Need Not Apply"), the more *every* woman is going to click away and look for someone who's not giving off toxic vibes.

Similarly, you need to nix any references to sex or seduction from your profile. If I had a dollar for every guy I've seen who has made a reference to how good he is in bed, his dick size, or his mastery of cunnilingus in his online dating profile, I'd be swimming through my money bin like Scrooge McDuck.

Pro tip: not only is nobody going to believe you, but you are also going to actively creep people out. The best you will be able to hope for is that you won't have people cruising by to point and laugh. If you have to advertise that you're good in bed… well, let's just say there's a reason why the confident don't feel the need to tell others. Irony, self-deprecating jokes or attempts at "edgy" humor can and *will* be misunderstood, especially in a text medium; unless you are very socially well-calibrated or extremely experienced in written humor, avoid them at all costs.

You also need to be aware of trends in dating profiles – especially ones to avoid, so as to not send the wrong message by mistake. Like it or not, fedoras, for example, have become synonymous with douchebags in online dating. No, it isn't fair that a handful of idiots have functionally turned a hat into the modern day equivalent of leprosy, but there's no point in protesting or complaining. If you wear a fedora in your online dating photo, people *are* going to judge you for it, no matter how much you protest that you're trying to reclaim it. The more you try to take a principled stand against some perceived dating injustice, the more your profile is going to end up serving as a warning to others.

Straight talk time: we are instinctively attracted to people who make us feel good. Positive, cheerful people are far more desirable as partners because they make *us* better. Negativity is unattractive, *especially* in a dating profile. The more shit you talk about people - individuals or groups - the less interested other people will be in *you*. As you put your profile together, remember: you're marketing yourself to others. Let them know how incredible you are and how much fun you are to be around.

---

[1] There is no "one". This person may be wonderful, but there are millions of people out there who, in the words of Tim Minchin, are statistically likely to be just as

nice.

² In fairness: most of the time, they'll get deluged in unwanted or undesired attention anyway; choosing "casual sex" just multiplies it exponentially.

³ Seriously: "Men Posing With Tigers" is its own genre on Tinder

⁴ So's "Men Wielding Fish". You want to impress women, not make them think you're saying "so I caught you a delicious bass".

⁵ Not a joke; I've seen all of these in use at one point or another

⁶ And believe me, no matter what "experts" and marketing gurus will tell you, it's more art than science.

⁷ OKCupid takes it a step farther with their match percentage heuristics; you can search by compatibility percentage, personality traits and questions answered. More on this later.

⁸ There is only one exception to this rule: when you're needing to fine-tune your profile. We'll cover this more in chapter 10.

Three

How To Look Good In Photos

Make Love To The Camera

The first step in building an online dating profile that gets results is often the hardest: choosing your profile photo. I don't know about you but I generally hate photos of myself. I can count the number of photos of myself that I like on the fingers of one hand - and most of *those* were taken by professionals. In fact, *lots* of people hate how they look in photos… which is a damned shame because they're a critical part of online dating.

We covered the importance of a good profile photo in the previous chapter, but to reiterate: your main profile photo is going to be the first thing that people check out. If they don't find it appealing, they're not going to continue on to view your profile, answer your messages or swipe right. But that doesn't mean that you need to look like Tyrese Gibson or Ryan Gosling or Sendhil Ramamurthy in order to find dating success. Looking good in photos isn't just about having perfect skin and cheekbones that could cut glass, it's about knowing how make the camera work for you. Looking good in photos is less about winning the genetic lottery and much more about skill - not just on the part of the model but on the photographer as well.

Despite what we may believe, the camera doesn't create a perfect record of reality. Not only are you trying to render a 3D figure in 2D space – which is going to skew proportions in a number of ways – but you're doing so through a series of refractive lenses and mirrors which introduce distortions. The list of things that affect how you appear in photos – ranging from the type of camera and lens to the lighting to the angle that you're facing – is immense. Even little things such as how far you stand from the camera, the film (or filter) in the camera, the focal length of the lens and even the tilt of your head can create profound differences in the final results. Much of a professional photographer's skill is understanding how all of these elements interplay with one another, how to correct for them and even how to make them work in the subject's favor.

And this is without getting into *psychological* aspects that affect the people who view your photos. Something as simple as wearing sunglasses can completely alter how people respond to you. When you understand a few tricks (and some common mistakes) you, too, can have the sort of dating profile photo that will have people flocking to your inbox.

DEVELOP THAT JAWLINE

Everyone's familiar with the adage "the camera adds ten pounds" - and it's entirely true. Everything I said about how cameras distort our shape and proportions leads to looking heavier in pictures. However, one of the biggest reasons for this effect, and the most easily correctable, has to do with the shape and angles of the face - specifically, the jaw. Many people don't take care to accentuate and define their jawline. When there's a lack of contrast between body parts, everything seems to blend together, giving the impression of squishiness. An undefined jawline means there isn't as much of a visual break between your face and your neck. As a result, you look soft and fleshy in ways you may find undesirable. A soft or undefined jaw can create the illusion of a double chin, even when you don't actually have one.

Now, to be sure, not all of us are blessed with the perfect bone structure that gives you a chiseled jawline, but there *are* ways to define and shape the jawline that don't end in reconstructive surgery or trying to reshape your face via Photoshop.

First, if you have a softer jaw or a not particularly prominent chin, then you may want to consider growing facial hair. A carefully maintained beard - or even some well cultivated stubble - can help provide visual contrast between your jawline and your neck. Different facial hair styles work better with different face shapes and sizes. A goatee or Van Dyke will help fill out a weak chin; letting it grow a little at the bottom helps fill in the space and lend some much needed symmetry. A short, neatly trimmed beard, on the other hand, can add shape and define your jawline and provide visual contrast between your jaw and neck, slimming down your facial profile.

Notice how I said "beard", not "chin-strap". Nobody likes the chinstrap. It makes you look like you've been trying to find a drummer for your Creed cover band and nobody wants that.

However, if you do this be sure that you keep your neck clean-shaven; hair or stubble on the underside of your jaw and neck can create the appearance of shadows that will soften up the contrast and undo the effect you were looking for.

Another trick you will want to employ is to use some simple poses that adjust your head's position to create greater separation between your jawline and your neck. Looking up can truncate your jaw, so you want to tilt your head down slightly to lengthen it. Next, imagine an invisible thread that's attached to the tip of your chin, tugging your head forward. Push your head forward ever so slightly. This brings your jaw out away from your neck, which creates a greater degree of definition and separation which creates more visual contrast.

And finally: if you have a slight double-chin or you're self-conscious about the softness under your chin and jaw, stick your tongue to the roof of your mouth. The ligaments in the underside of your tongue will pull the flesh upwards and smooth things out.

DON'T HIDE YOUR EYES

You've heard the cliche that "the eyes are the window to the soul" before. It's 100% true. Eye contact is a critical form of non-verbal communication in humans; it's an instinctive part of how we signal interest, improve cooperation or even alert others to danger. Under the right circumstances, strong eye contact can even cause us to fall in love. Eye contact is *just* that powerful and meaningful - so much so that when we *can't* make eye-contact with someone, we get uncomfortable around them. Not being able to see someone's eyes – or they won't make eye contact with us – is disconcerting because it feels deceptive; if we can't see their eyes, how do we know whether or not we can trust them? *Not* meeting someone's eyes is one of the classic tells of whether somebody is lying or hiding something after all…

This is why you don't want to put barriers to eye-contact in your photos - especially in your main profile photo. In fact, this is hands-down one of the most consistent mistakes I see in online dating photos. If you want to look good in photos, you have to make sure that people can see your eyes clearly. The harder people have to work to see your eyes, the less likely they are to respond positively to your profile.

The biggest mistake people make is wearing sunglasses. Now, I get the intent; you want to look cool, even a little mysterious, and nothing says "cool, brooding bad-ass celebrity" like a sweet pair of shades, right? In practice, that sense of "cool" just means that people will like you less. Studies have shown that people are much less likely to respond positively to photos of people in sunglasses[1]. It's putting a barrier between you and the person you're hoping to connect with, making you appear less likable and less approachable. You also want to avoid other effects that inadvertently obscure your eyes. Deep shadows, for example, have a similar effect to sunglasses. This is one more reason you want to leave your fedora[2] off in your dating profile photos; the brim casts unflattering shadows over your eyes. Similarly, props that cover your eyes – whether it's holding up the phone in the "taking my self-portrait in the mirror"[3] pose to letting your hair fall over your face – detract from the message you're trying to send. And while we're talking about the eyes…

USE THE "SQUINCH"

Part of what makes someone look good in photos? Confidence. One trick to remember is that confidence isn't just in how you feel, it's in how you *carry* yourself. Most of human communication is done non-verbally; seemingly little things like the slope of your shoulders, the tilt of your head and the angle of your eyes all carry volumes of information, context and meaning that words alone do *not*. Moreover, your body language gives away information about how you're feeling. Even little changes in posture and expression tell outside observers whether you're feeling confident or scared. It's in the the way you stand, the way you carry yourself, the expression on your face… even the way you squint.

Wait, what?

Remember how I was saying that the eyes are key to communication? They are also part of how we signal our emotional states to others. When we're being sarcastic or feeling frustrated with someone, we roll our eyes. When we're happy, it shows in our eyes. When we're angry and confrontational, we'll stare somebody down. The literal look in your eye will affect how people think of you, and that effect comes through in photographs. Think of how many times you've seen someone do the "Deer In The Headlights" look in a photo. At best, it looks silly. At worst, they look like they're terrified out of their goddamned mind. When your eyes are wide – showing the whites of your eyes, as it were – you're signaling surprise, fear and uncertainty… not exactly emotions you want to project in a dating profile photo. Slightly narrowing your eyes, on the other hand, reverses the effect; you're displaying greater levels of confidence.

Seem crazy? OK, stick with me for a second, because there's actually a point behind this.

One of the most common ways of showing confidence, openness and friendliness is through a smile. A genuine smile – also known as a "Duchenne" smile – is a smile that crinkles up your face. One of the keys to telling a genuine smile from a fake smile is to watch the eyes; a genuine smile makes the corners of your eyes crinkle up and causes you to squint slightly.

Portrait photographer Peter Hurley came up with the concept of what he calls "the squinch" as a way of looking more confident and self-assured in photos. The squinch is a very simple trick: you lift and tighten your lower eyelids while letting your top eyelids droop slightly. When done correctly, you're replicating the way that your eyes crinkle during a Duchenne smile. And it *works*; the blog Photofeeler found that photos of subjects doing the squinch were all rated as being more self-assured, more influential and more competent. It's a very little thing that yields powerful results.

Just remember: its a "squinch", not a "squint". You're trying to look more confident, not doing your best Clint Eastwood impression or looking like you're staring into the sun. If you're having a hard time perfecting your squinch, check YouTube; Peter Hurley has a video specifically about doing the squinch.

Show Your Torso

One of the keys to taking amazing photographs is framing and cropping – understanding how much to show and how much to leave out. The way you frame a photo can affect how people respond to it emotionally; you're using everything from the background to the shape of the photograph to highlight and draw the viewer's attention to the subject of the image.

When we're applying this to dating profile photos, framing and cropping means understanding just how much of yourself to display.

Hang on, that came out wrong. Let me try that again.

When you're picking photos for an online dating profile, you want to present an accurate (albeit flattering) portrayal of how you look, which is why body shots are important. However, studies have found that showing your *whole* body actually makes the photo *less* attractive. In order to include your whole body, the photographer has to increase the amount of distance from the camera to the subject, which in turn creates a

The Guide To Mastering Online Dating

feeling of distance between the subject and the *viewer*.

So how much should you show? Over at PhotoFeeler, after studying 60,000 ratings of 800 photographs, they found that people respond most favorably to torso shots and busts[4], and less so to full-body photos and head-only pics. Let's compare these two photos of the same model. Same pose, same lighting, but one's predominantly torso while the other is full-body:

The second photo – featuring the model's full body – has less impact than the first. Because it's so zoomed out, it distances the subject from the viewer. Yeah, you can see his entire body and be assured that he's not wandering around on oddly stubby chicken legs, but it you're losing a *lot* of important visual detail.

The closer photo on the other hand shows enough of the body to give an accurate idea of how he looks while still being close enough to foster a greater sense of intimacy with the model. You're able to see more of his face and those all-important eyes; they're far too small and hard to make out in the full-body shot. A shot of just the head, on the other hand, doesn't convey the same level of information; you get what their face looks like but that's it. In fact, a dating profile with nothing *but* face shots tends to make people on dating sites feel as though you're trying to hide unflattering features. A bust shot[5] conveys more information, and has been a staple of art and portraiture since antiquity. And if it's good enough for Roman emperors, it's good enough for you.

CONTROL THE LIGHTING

If you want to look good in photos, you need to control the light. Any photographer will tell you: manipulating the light source will completely change how you look. Let's look at two photos involving the same model using two very different light setups:

This photo is relatively neutral - it says "Hey honey, I'm going to the store on the way home, should I get something?"

The Guide To Mastering Online Dating

This photo, however, screams "I WANT TO LICK THE INSIDE OF YOUR RIBCAGE, CLAIRICE."

Notice how dramatically different the model looks: an adjustment in the angle of the light causes wrinkles to appear deeper, creases get emphasized, pores and bumps stand out more, the skin texture is rougher and he has bags under his eyes when he didn't have any before.

Just changing the *direction* of the light source not only creates a vastly different mood, but completely changes the topography of the face.

Everything about light, from the angle, the source, how even the coverage is, whether it's diffused or not... all of these can make dramatic differences in how you look in photos. The ideal light for photos is indirect sunlight, preferably either shortly after sunrise or shortly before sunset – these are known as the golden hours. Of course, not all of us can arrange to have photos taken only at times when the light is perfect, so it's important to understand which forms of lighting can make you look like a million bucks and how to minimize light that makes you look bad.

Indirect light - that is, light from multiple angles or sources, where the light is evenly balanced on all sides - is the best. Indirect light minimizes shadows, which brings out the smoothness in the face and skin. Direct light - light from a single source that only illuminates one side of the subject - is almost always a bad idea for dating photos. Direct light can create harsh shadows that get read as wrinkles and pits, and overly-bright highlights make your skin look shiny and greasy. This is why photos with on-camera flash tend to look awful – it's a bright, direct light that washes you out and gives you a massive case of red-eye.

Overhead direct light - such as from under a bright ceiling light - is especially bad; it ensures long, dramatic shadows that will warp your proportions and make you look "off" at best and outright sinister at worst.

The *type* of light matters as well - different light sources produce different qualities of light. Candlelight creates a soft warm glow that can feel romantic or seductive. Soft light bulbs create a more diffuse, flattering light while standard clear bulbs can give a harsh, yellow cast to everything. LED lights have a very "cold" light that can make the subject look washed out and pale.

The worst lighting for pictures, however, is *fluorescent* lighting. Those long humming tubes that illuminate your office may be cheap and use less electricity, but the light makes your skin look sickly and sallow while bringing out any blemishes you may have while highlighting any unevenness in your skin tone. Ever wonder why your reflection looks god-awful when you're trying on clothes at the mall? Nine times out of ten, you're dealing with overhead fluorescent lighting - a perfect combination to make you look like a plague-ridden zombie. Remember: fluorescent lighting is *never* your friend.

KNOW YOUR ANGLES

Have you ever heard someone talk about "shooting them from their good side?" Did you roll your eyes a little when they said it? Did you think that they were being a little over-dramatic, a little too model-wanna-be? Guess what? They actually know what they're talking about. As it turns out, your "good side" is actually a thing.

Most people don't have perfectly symmetrical faces (Shania Twain and Denzel Washington being the apparent exceptions). All of us have features that aren't perfectly aligned, centered or even; your nose might be slightly larger on one side, your mouth might be slightly lopsided or one eye might be higher than the other. Even Hollywood celebrities will have features that are just noticeably off true - *Teen Wolf's* Tyler Posey has an crooked chin while Shannen Doherty and Kat Graham both famously have eyes that are uneven.

This facial asymmetry is part of why we're often surprised by how we look in photos versus how we look in the mirror. We're *used* to how we look in the mirror - we've seen it so many times that it seems normal to us. But photos don't shoot our mirror images and so we're frequently seeing ourselves at an angle that we're unused to. As a result: we find them a little off-putting. But if you know it's there, then you can correct for it.

Yes, you could always use the Liquify tool in Photoshop to fix those imperfections, but people who seem relentlessly photogenic understand which angles show them in the best light. They make a point of posing posing such a way that any asymmetries are minimized or disguised. One of the easiest ways to find your "good" side is to simply turn your head to the side and present a three-quarters profile. You don't want to turn more than 30 degrees; past that point, not only do you start looking like you're looking at something off camera, but you get a foreshortening effect that you don't want. A slight tilt of the head in one direction or the other can also minimize any asymmetric features. Just remember, it's a *slight* tilt; too much and you start looking like a dog wondering what its master just said.

It can take some time to find your "good" side – you may need to take a few selfies or go through photos with a friend in order to figure out which angle suits you best. But when you do, you'll have photos that'll grab people's attention and get them clicking on your profile in order to know more.

[1] Interestingly, studies indicate that people respond *more* positively to people who wear eyeglasses. The cultural context of eyeglasses (they make you look smarter) outweighs the barrier effect.

[2] Well, *any* brimmed hat, but especially the fedora, trilby, homburg and any other old-time-y hat in that general family.

Except bowlers. Bowler hats are cool.

[3] Again: no mirror selfies!

[4] They mean pictures of the head and shoulders, not boobs.

[5] Ho ho, ha ha. Very funny.

FOUR

BUILDING THE PERFECT PROFILE

A NOTE ABOUT BUILDING YOUR PROFILE

When it comes to dating, the age-old question is "what matters more: looks or personality?" And as it turns out, we have an answer: personality wins in the long run. Don't get me wrong: good looks help... but "good looking" is a hell of a moving target. The attractive power of physical looks changes rather drastically over time. While being stunningly good looking helps with *initial* impressions, its value levels off very quickly and becomes much less important over time while other factors increase dramatically. In fact, scientific studies from the University of Texas at Austin have found that desirability and attraction is about more than appearance - it's about *personality*.[1]

Your dating profile is going to be what makes or breaks your dating experience. Your photos are what get you in the door. Your *profile* is what seals the deal.

Before we get started with creating *your* profile, you should take a look around at some *other* people's profiles, especially for people who live in your area. These are the people who're in the same dating pool as you. Some of them will inspire you. More of them will serve as examples of what *not* to do. You may notice how *similar* they all are. This is why you want to make sure you stand out from them and let your profile shine.

Now a quick caveat: as I said last time, I prefer OKCupid to most dating sites out there, especially pay sites. Therefore I'll be talking predominantly about OK Cupid's profile set-up. If you want to go with Match, Zoosk, Plenty of Fish, Chemistry, Geek2Geek, Farmers Only, what-have-you, that's cool. There's a certain universality to most dating site profiles these days and the concepts transfer even if the exact details don't.

Now let's get started.

PROFILE WRITING BEST PRACTICES

While you're writing your profile, you want to keep two ideas in mind. First: keep it concise. You don't want to write a novel in your self-summary; people aren't going to want to have to dig through your rhetorical flourishes to get to the meat. Just because you're given 1000 characters doesn't mean you need to use *all* of them. Past a certain point - 100 words, according to some studies - people will TL;DR and move on. Give more than a tweet's worth of information, but try to think Hemingway, not Faulkner. Short, punchy sentences work best.

The other thing is to remember to be interesting. You don't need to be impressive, overwhelming people with your accomplishments, you need to be *relatable*. Give the people who visit your profile something to respond to, little hooks or keywords for them to focus on. Don't be vague or offer generalities - provide *specifics*. You like to read? OK fine, *what* do you like to read? Not just genre but specific titles or authors. You like to take walks out in the forest? *Why*? Do you like the feel of the sun on your skin, the smell of the wildflowers, the peace of getting away from the city for a little while? Do you appreciate the hum of traffic late at night? These are all concrete things that people can latch on to as well as give them a sense of who you are. They round you out as a person and give insight to why you're interesting.

Straight talk: attitude is *everything*. A shitty

attitude is going to turn people off and make them wonder why you're on here. They'll worry that if they write you, they'll get a series of creepy or angry ranting emails in reply. If someone reads your profile and gets the impression that you're sad, angry or resentful, they're going to "NEXT!" you so hard your head will spin. Instead, you want to convey three universally attractive traits: you're positive, approachable and confident. These three traits will make you more appealing to just about everyone who reads your profile, no matter whether you're an introvert or an extrovert, shy or outgoing, a home-body or a person who likes to go out every night of the week.

See, people instinctively *like* people who make us feel good; the more that we enjoy ourselves in their presence, the more we'll want to spend time with them. This is known as the Reward Theory of Attraction - we prioritize the relationships that are emotionally satisfying and gratifying. Someone who's relentlessly negative sucks the energy out of the room and makes people around them feel drained, while someone who's positive *gives* energy to others; thus we want to spend the most time around positive people. Approachability signals that you're friendly and open and less likely to reject somebody off the bat. The aloof, superior snarky persona of a Dr. House or Sherlock Holmes makes for great characters but in real life, they're miserable little shits that nobody in their right mind would want to talk to; how eager would *you* be to try to strike up a conversation with someone if you thought they were going to respond to everything with sarcasm and withering putdowns?

Another thing to keep in mind is that the messed up gender roles that dictate how men and women socialize tend to follow us online. The same negative social messaging that tells women to be passive and not to make the first move affects how women use online dating as well. Many women have experienced approaching a guy and having him either freak out and call her a slut or assume that she is *far* more interested than she actually is. Out in person, you can use body language and approach invitations to signal your being open to women approaching you. In online dating, you don't have those options; what you *do* have is your words. By making sure you come across as friendly and approachable in your profile, you're helping encourage women to message *you* first.

This is also why you should avoid adding hurdles or challenges to potential matches. Creating more work for people by saying things like "Google it" when you make an obscure reference or insisting that people should do X, Y or Z to talk to you just means that they're going to move on. I'm going to be blunt here: *nobody* is going to be so invested in you that they're going to go out of their way to jump through hoops for you. They have better things to do and frankly the ones who *do* are almost always people you'd rather not date in the first place.

Confidence should be fairly self-explanatory: confidence is *sexy*. However, people often confuse arrogance or ego for confidence, especially in online dating. Many people assume that their profile has to show that they are the hottest, most impressive thing in the history of man and that need to outshine every other guy out there. This is a mistake; you don't need to be superhuman to be desirable, you just need to be secure in yourself. Someone who uses wishy-washy language with lots of hedge statements and weasel words ("I guess I'm...", "People say that I...") or passive language come across as needy and insecure. *Own* your profile. Make it fun. Show that you're looking for a partner, not someone to reassure you or prop up your ego. The more self-assured you are in your profile, the more attractive you'll be.

Remember what I said earlier about your brand. Your profile is where you're putting yourself on display for other people's judgement. People are going to form emotional associations based around what you have to say, and those associations are going to affect whether or not they want to talk with you.

Don't worry: I'll give you some tips on how to shape those associations and display your best, most *authentic* self.

Don't Try To Appeal To Everyone

There's a phrase I see crop up in "inspirational" memes on Tumblr and Facebook: "I'd Rather Be Someone's Shot of Whiskey Instead of Everyone's Cup of Tea". As much as the twee-ness of it makes me gag, it does make a good point.

One of the most common mistakes that I see people make is that they have crafted their online dating profiles to be as broadly appealing as possible. Now I realize that this seems a little counter-intuitive; after all, don't you want to appeal to more people? The wider you cast your net, the more fish you haul in, right?

The problem with this approach is that by trying to appeal to everyone, you end up appealing to *no one*. You're catering to the lowest common denominator and, as a result, losing anything that makes you appealing, unique or different. You've made your profile so broad that your personality fell out and all that's left is a bland mush. It's not surprising; a lot of people take the tack of trying to avoid rejection and to refrain from displaying any common deal-breakers. It becomes an exercise in saying what you *aren't*, rather than what you *are*. If the best thing that you can say about your profile is that it's inoffensive, then you shouldn't be surprised by your stunning lack of success.

Trying to appeal to too many people at once means that you're spending a lot of time and effort for minimal return. Since all of online dating is, at its core, marketing, you have to think like a marketer. Do you want to appeal to a broad audience, and one that's saturated with competitors at that, or do you want to target a smaller, more niche audience that is actively looking for what you have to offer? That broad audience, while tempting, is a mistake; a large demographic that thinks you're ok or nice enough is far less likely to respond to your messages than a smaller demo that *really* digs what you have to offer.

This means you have to be willing to be polarizing when it comes to your dating profile. You have to be willing to have strong opinions and to let your personality shine through, even if it means that you'll potentially be cutting yourself off from a wider base of potential matches. Are you a Whovian with strong opinions about the Moffat era vs. the Davies era? Make that known – other sci-fi geeks are going to want to find you, even if the supposed "cool" kids think you're weird. If you're a Brony, go ahead and let people know. The people who're going to give you shit for loving *Friendship is Magic* aren't going to suddenly be more tolerant of it when you surprise them with it later, and you end up missing out on fellow fans of the show. If you're only looking for a casual relationship, say so; don't be the douchebag who pretends to be interested in something long-term just because you don't want to scare people off. Similarly, if you only want a relationship that's going to lead to kids and the white-picket-fences of suburban living, make that clear. Let your best, most authentic self shine through in your profile, even if that means not everyone's going to like it.

By that same token, however, you'll want to avoid mentioning the things you're *not* into. It may seem a little counter-intuitive, but it's part and parcel of the dating SEO; people search by keywords, and those searches *don't* check for context. If you have a line in your self-summary about how you're not willing to date a single parent, you're going to show up in searches for the phrase "single parent" - bringing people who you're not interested to your profile and from there into your inbox. Attention is great, but attention from people who you're not compatible with is useless and annoying.

Yes, it can hard to be willing to put yourself out there, knowing that some folks aren't going to like you. But trying to avoid rejection just ensures that you're going to be bland and undesirable. Not everybody loves whiskey. Many people will never touch the stuff. But the people who do? They *love* it.

You don't want people who think you're just ok.

You want to be the thing they *crave*.

THE VITAL STATISTICS

Every dating site is going to include certain statistics at the bare minimum. Even if all they give you is 500 characters to describe yourself, they're *still* going to ask for the basics: height, weight, body type, hair color[2], etc. These are going to form the majority of the search parameters that people use to find matches, and many sites allow their users to restrict people who fall outside of a certain range. Others, such as Match, will compare your stats to what she says she's looking for and show where you match up and where you don't.

Using OKCupid as our model, you'll be asked to

define:

- Sexual orientation
- Ethnicity
- Height
- Body Type
- Diet (carnivore, vegetarian, vegan, kosher, halal, etc)
- Smoke
- Drinks
- Drug use
- Religion (and how strict you are about it)
- Your Astrological Sign (and how seriously you take it)
- Your educational level
- Your job (type/industry)
- Your Income Level
- Relationship Status
- Relationship Type (monogamous, non-monogamous)
- Kids (have any/want any)

- Pets (what you like/what you have)
- Languages

For the most part, this is fairly straight forward. However, there's a certain temptation to, shall we say, "fudge" things a little when it comes to your statistics, a little resume padding if you will. While it's understandable - and God knows most people do it - I'd recommend against it. One of the points of online dating is to actually *meet* people who you're compatible with, whether you're hoping to settle down and get married or simply to find someone to hook up with on the weekend. Throwing misinformation into the mix in hopes of increasing the number of potential matches (or not *decreasing* them) only makes it harder to meet the *right* people.

Most forms of resume padding - increasing your height by an inch or two or nudging up your income level - is fairly minor but still fundamentally dishonest[3] and often means that you're meeting people who are searching for things you don't have Others - such as choosing "fit" or "athletic" when you're demonstrably *not* - are going to be immediately clear when you meet in person and that's going to piss that person off. I get that you may not be an Adonis; 99% of the population isn't. You aren't going to disguise this fact by choosing the wrong option and all you're doing is setting up a ticking time-bomb that's counting down to the moment when they realize you tried to fool them. When in doubt, choose "average" and just let your photos do the talking for you.

Fudging on other stats - such as suggesting that you want kids when you don't or aren't really sure or listing yourself as monogamous when you aren't - just ensures that you're going to end up meeting people whose priorities are different from yours. Again: you're standing in the way of your own goals; you're trying to meet people who you *click* with, not just rack up profile visits.

Some stats are, by their nature, going to be more vital than others. Most people aren't going to stress too much if you don't mention that you're a Pisces or what languages you speak; the odds that somebody is looking for a partner who specifically speaks Esperanto is fairly low. Not having an answer on, say, income level or job, on the other hand, comes across as your trying to hide a feature that you know will turn people off. Similarly not having an answer at *all* on things like "height" or "sexual orientation" means you won't show up in some people's searches.

I get that you may not want to miss out on

potential matches, but having more people respond to your profile isn't going to do you any good if the jig will be up as soon as you meet in person.

FILLING OUT YOUR SUMMARY

Now we get to the meat of your dating profile - your self-summary. Your story. The part where you describe who you are and what you're all about and why people should want to get to know you in person. This is where you want to polish up your image to a lovely shine. This is *also* the place where all the interest people have shown in you can fall apart. The point of your profile is to sell yourself - but you have to know how to do it *right*. People tend to assume that when they're being honest about themselves, they have to present things as plainly as possible. This is a mistake; you can be perfectly honest but *still* display yourself in your best light. It's all about attitude and word choice, delivered in short, meaty chunks.

Let's use OKCupid's profile as a template and break it all down, shall we?

Your self-summary:

Who are you, why do I want to talk to you? This is your opening argument, who you are in a nutshell.

You want to paint a picture of your life that your matches are going to want to be part of. You don't need to be Captain Adventure, diving out of airplanes one week and exploring the Amazon the next[4], you just have to be somebody that like-minded people would want to spend time with. What is it about you that makes you interesting? No, the answer is *not* "nothing". What drives you? What are you passionate about? What makes you get excited to get up in the morning? These are the things you want to emphasize; passion and drive is attractive, even if you're convinced that nobody else would find it interesting. *Everything* is fascinating if you explain just *why* you love it and what makes it so special to you. Resist the urge to make self-deprecating jokes - unless you're *extremely* obvious about it, people will believe you're completely serious. Similarly, don't pretend that you're above all this. This is the 21st century. Everyone lives their lives online now and this includes finding love. Pretending that you're somehow superior to everyone else just makes you look like an asshole.

What are you doing with your life:

This is where you talk about what you do. Most people tend to launch straight into what they do for a living. If you have an awesome job that you're proud of, then gush a little bit. On the other hand, if your job isn't anything special - just the way you're keeping body and soul together - then talk a little about your life and ambitions instead. It's all in how you describe it: if you're a photographer, then say "I take photos of cool people." If you hike or like doing outdoor activities, you might say "exploring the great outdoors every chance I get". If you travel a lot, say "I'm trying to get every page on my passport stamped" or "Trying to visit every state in the country."

What you're good at:

This is a place to be fun and playful. It's also a license to brag, just a little, so if you have some notable accomplishments, then this is the place for it. Just remember: anyone can say whatever they want… that doesn't mean that people will believe you. Saying that you're funny or have a great sense of humor isn't going to convince anyone. *Show* them that you're funny; make a joke, be silly, give them an example of your sense of humor. Going a little over the top is acceptable here as long as it's clear you're exaggerating for humorous effect - if you cook, say you make the best *duck a l'orange* anyone has ever tasted.

Just be aware of how you come across. Giving Sensitive Nice Guy answers like "being a great listener" just says "I will bring you Häagen-Daz and kleenex and let you regale me with tales of the latest asshole who dumped you while I secretly yearn to get in your pants." It's called "online *dating*" not "online faking being your friend until I can catch you in a moment of weakness." Talking about sex *at all* here - whether you're bragging or making fun of yourself - is going to make you seem creepy. Humor can cover for a number of sins, but remember: the fail state of "clever" is "asshole."

The first thing people notice about me:

Unless you have something that really stands out - visible tattoos, lots of piercings, you're over 6 feet tall, you wear an eyepatch - then you can be a little silly here. "My piercing blue eyes and the fact that ninjas are shadowing my every move, waiting to strike," has worked for me.

Favorite Books, Movies, Shows, Music and Food

This is designed to provide commonalities and conversational hooks between you and anyone you message (or who may message you), not to list every favorite you have. List a few specific titles or names for each category and move on. If you don't have a particular favorite - you don't watch much TV, say -

then make an obvious joke and move to the next category.

Six things I can't do without:

First of all: Maslow's Hierarchy of Needs has been done. By me. Then every other smart-ass on OKCupid got in on the action and now it's played out. So has "oxygen", "food" and other obvious choices. Don't dither or apologize about how you only have three things or how you could barely cut it down to six. Just list things that give some insight into your personality and interests and move on.

I spend a lot of time thinking about:

This is where damn near *everybody* falls into one of two camps[5]: either they try to sound deep and soulful or they mention something absurdly boring. Nobody is going to believe that you spend time contemplating Herman Hesse or pondering the plight of children in the third world. Unless you have some serious activist cred, avoid trying to sound like you're trying to save the world. And to be honest, most people aren't going to care about this section anyway, so I say go over the top. Personally, I recommend something along the lines of "19th Century Russian Literature. All of it." or "Latvian Tractor Porn".

On a typical Friday night I am:

This question isn't as much about "what do you do on a typical Friday night" and more "what kind of person are you looking for?" This is where you separate the introverts from the extroverts and the bar-hoppers from the museum visitors. This question tells people what you like to do in your free time and gives an idea of what a date with you would be like. As tempting as it is to make yourself sound like a super-popular, always in demand kind of guy, getting too flippant here means that you'll be selling yourself to people you're not actually interested in.

There are three things to avoid. First: there's nothing more generic than "I like to go out with friends, but sometimes I like a night at home." Congratulations: you just described the entire human population. I suppose you like to eat "food" too. Second: "Out with you, hopefully" is both stupid *and* desperate. Never do this. And third: no matter what you do, do *not* give the impression that you don't have a life. People who read your profile are wondering what life with you would be like. If you don't do *anything*, they'll look for someone who's life revolves around more than collecting dust on the couch. This doesn't mean that homebodies are out of luck - just describe a low-key date that you'd like to go on.

The most private thing I'm willing to admit:

Let's be real: nobody's admitting anything terribly private here. Once again, it's a place to be silly. Make shit up. If you have some deep and dark secret that people need to know, then it's better to share that in a message before the two of you meet in person so they can make up their mind.

You Should Message Me If:

The subtext of this question isn't "you should message me", it's "this is the type of person I'm looking for". You're giving an indication of the personality type that you click with in a partner. List a few of the *non-physical* qualities that you want in a date - things like "you're adventurous" or "you love to read". It's also a good place to indicate potential activities: "You should message me if you want to get coffee and talk about how awesome *Daredevil* is" or "You're looking for someone who will go dancing until dawn."

There are two bad answers here: first is "if you want to". Believe me, nobody is going to be messaging you because they *don't* want to but are somehow compelled by horrible eldritch forces from beyond the outer dark. It's stupid and obvious. The other bad answer is to list reasons why people *shouldn't* message you - all of your deal breakers, resentments and lists of them as what done you wrong. It's not a good look on you.

Once you've finished your profile, sleep on it. Come back the next day and proof-read it. Are you making sure to include the right keywords? Are your descriptions as lean and tight as they can be or can you trim the fat a little more? If you were a total stranger, what would you think of the person who wrote this? Are you coming across as someone fun to hang around with? It may help to get a second - or even a third - set of eyes to look things over and give you an outsider's opinion.

Just remember: your profile is never "finished" because *you* are never finished. You're always growing, changing and improving, and you should adjust your profile to match. Don't be afraid to adjust and rewrite things regularly; adjusting your profile helps keep you visible in searches.

---

[1] I go into this more in my other books: *New Game +* and *Simplified Dating* - available in ebook format now!

[2] The exception, of course, being Tinder, which only gives your photos and a brief "about me". Which is why half the time, one of the first questions people get on Tinder is "how tall are you?"

[3] I *do* make a slight exception for height and relationship status under specific circumstances - more about that in Chapter 10.

[4] Although if you *are*, make sure you include photos of you doing said jumping and exploring.

[5] The exception to this are the stoners. But they try to work "weed" into *everything*.

Five

Making Contact

Avoid The Telemarketer Approach

One of the leading causes of frustration with online dating is the pain of sending out email after email and never hearing back. You're putting all of this effort into each message and casting it out into the void with nothing to show for it but the dull ache as another piece of your soul withers away and dies of loneliness. That empty inbox becomes yet another mocking reminder that you're doomed to die alone, unloved and unmourned.

Therein lies the problem: you're putting in all of that effort for no return. It's part of the cold calculus of online dating: most people aren't going to respond to your messages, whether you're a man or a woman. To be perfectly blunt: you're wasting your time and energy by messaging the wrong people and in the wrong way.

A man writing a email to a woman with no previous contact or flirtation has a 25% chance of getting a reply[1].

As I laid out in my book Simplified Dating, I'm a big believer in efficiency when it comes to dating. Meeting women - whether in person or online - is more fun and more satisfying when you're not spending time and energy needlessly. You may be familiar with the Pareto Principle: 20% of your effort give you 80% of your results. When it comes to online dating, that 20% comes from your profile and messaging people the *right* way.

When most people join an online dating site, they've basically become the dating equivalent of a telemarketer. Emailing potential matches is functionally the same as cold-calling a marketing lead; you're trying to connect with a stranger and convince them to check out your product. The only difference here is that your product is, well, you. And the person you're trying to connect with has received dozens of calls from *other* telemarketers already within the last three hours. It's not surprising, then, that she's going to react the way most of us do when telemarketers call: by screening her calls and pretending to not be home.

Now, to be fair: a shotgun approach to online

dating is certainly *one* way of meeting people. Throw enough out there and you'll hit something *eventually*. Hell, some people right-swipe *everyone* on Tinder in order to maximize the odds that they'll have a match.

The problem with this method should be obvious: you're putting yourself out there over and over again, expending all of that time and energy for little to no reward. It's exhausting. It's demoralizing. And it's inefficient. You're sending out dozens, even *hundreds* of messages every day to every profile that catches your eye in hopes of getting at least one or two messages.

That's a recipe for frustration and burn-out if ever there was one.

The problem with using the telemarketer approach with online dating is very simple: you're messaging people who haven't shown any interest in you. They have no reason to read your message; when you're cold-calling a woman's dating profile you're just one more person in a sea of people clamoring for her attention. The odds of their choosing to read *your* message out of *all* of the ones they get is fairly low. To make matters worse, women frequently get flooded with absolutely *shitty* messages from guys - guys who are too old or too young or who live too far away, guys who are a lousy match and the constant refrain of "u want sum fuck?" punctuated with the occasional "Fuck you bitch you're not hot enough to treat me like this." Dealing with that level of bullshit every day is grueling; many women will frequently trash every email that seems even slightly dodgy without reading them... and your perfectly polite and respectful message may well get caught up in the purge.

If you want better results from your dating profile, you need to learn how to message people strategically. Yes, taking the shotgun approach and blasting out messages has its place, but it shouldn't be where you focus your energy. You're having to build their interest in you from zero - or worse, from negative values. That's a *lot* of effort to put in for minimal return. If you want more success and more responses, then you want to prioritize sending messages to the people who are most likely to write back: the ones who show interest in *you*.

This is why a carefully written profile is so important. If you've been following my advice, then your profile should be doing the lion's share of the work for you - people should be finding you in their searches and be intrigued enough to take a closer look to see what you've got going on. Every dating site out there will show you the most recent visitors to your profile; some, like OKCupid, offer paid features that give you even more information on who's been checking you out. These are the people you should be focusing your attention on. By reading your profile, they've shown that they are at least a *little* curious about you. That curiosity drastically raises the likelihood that they'll read and respond to your messages.

The higher the level of interest they show, the higher a priority they should be when it comes to messaging people. Someone who sent you a message first is *very* interested, someone who rates your profile or sends a wink or a nudge is slightly less so and someone who visited your page without saying anything is slightly less than that. The frequency of visits is also an indication of interest - if you've noticed that they've visited your profile a couple of times, they're likely psyching themselves up to say something.

However, don't assume that just because they didn't send a message that they aren't interested in hearing from you - some people are shy, while others are browsing and bookmarking potential matches for later. If someone viewed your profile, check *them* out, decide if you like what you see and then send them a quick "I noticed you noticing me" message.

Save your energy; you should use the shotgun

approach sparingly. Cold-calling should make up less than 30% of your time on dating sites. Focus your energy on messaging people who're interested in you, and keeping your profile interesting and visible.

Don't worry: we'll cover tips and tricks to maximize your profile's visibility in later chapters in the book.

But while we're talking about online dating time-wasters…

Don't Send Winks, Pokes or Flirts

Remember how I said you should message people who send you a wink or a nudge? That only goes one way. Confused? Allow me to explain:

Almost every dating site out there has some form of a low-stakes "hey, so and so wants you to talk to them" notification. These are usually given a cutsey name like "wink" or "flirt" or "send a flower" to make it seem appealing or part of the dating process. The problem is that, quite frankly, they *don't work*.

(Well… kind of. I'll get to the exceptions in a moment.)

Before we get into why winks and nudges are a

losing game, let me tell you a story about the early days of Internet dating. Back in those dark days of the late 90's and early 00's, dating sites relied less on subscription fees and more on selling you access to other people's profiles on a piecemeal basis. Sites would let you create profiles, but if you wanted to actually contact somebody, you had to pay up. In order to message someone you were interested in, you had to buy credits; it would cost you one credit in order to message a profile for the first time; if they responded, then you could message each other back and forth freely. Some were especially evil and would require that you spend a credit for *each email*; if you sent out a message and didn't hear back, well, tough shit Charlie, you just blew a buck (or whatever the per-unit cost was). Winks, nudges, flowers, etc. were intended as a way of trying to get someone to message *you*, so that you could chat without wasting your hard-earned money. Needless to say, it was kind of insulting even back then; nothing screams "romance" more than "I'm interested in you but not enough to actually pay to join the site."

These days, pay sites have wised up; the vast majority[2] charge a flat subscription fee that allows unlimited messaging to everyone, but the vestigial organ that is the "wink" hangs in there like an appendix and does nothing but cause trouble.

Here's the thing you need to understand: women tend to get a raw deal when it comes to online dating. Yes, they get a lot of attention, but that's rarely attention that they actually *want*. It's bad enough for a woman to be getting email after email from people who clearly haven't read her profile and who only think of her as a pair of tits and a vagina to perform for their pleasure. Having someone say "I know you're probably not going to write back if I wrote to you so please do the hard work for me!" is just adding insult to injury. It's not cute and flirty, it's betraying a lack of confidence at best and passive-aggressive at worst. Throw that on top of the gender roles that *still* insist men have to be the aggressors and you end up with a system that actively discourages women from being more proactive.

As a result: winks and nudges and the like are a loser's game for men when it comes to online dating. Women have better results using them simply because men are more likely to respond in general. No, it's *not* fair. Yes, it's a total double-standard. Blame society for this one, but in the meantime, you have to deal with the world the way it is.

Now for the exception to the "no winks" rule:

Some sites have the opportunity for you to "like" or rate someone anonymously; if you like each other, then the site tells you both. If not they never know.[3] Tinder's whole design is based on this method. This can be a useful secondary method of contacting people, since the anonymity helps eliminate the "notice me noticing you" factor unless there's mutual interest. However, your mileage may vary. Some people love quick-match features; some find them less than useless. Play around with it and see how you feel about the results.

MAKING THE FIRST MESSAGE COUNT

There are a number of competing philosophies when it comes to messages in online dating. Some insist that you should be the proactive searcher, seeking out as many profiles as possible and messaging them. Others believe in being as passive as possible and letting *them* come to *you*. There are benefits and drawbacks to both approaches - searchers expend a *lot* of energy trying to connect but reach a greater number of people, receivers have less control over who they hear from but have greater levels of responses. Personally, I believe in achieving a mix of the two - a willingness to be proactive helps you exercise more discretion and helps cut down on low-quality matches, while an attractive and well-written profile invites other people to message *you*.

But if you're going to be making the first move - whether you're cold-messaging somebody or you're initiating contact with someone who's already shown interest - then you need to make those messages count.

Writing messages on a dating site is an art form, but one that many people don't quite understand. See, many people assume that their message is what gets them the date. Some people put their heart and soul into each electronic missive they send out into the digital ether. Others try to adapt pick-up artist tricks like negging[4] or compliance tests[5] in order to try to manipulate the recipient into writing back. Some play the suck-up who showers the other person in complements, while others take the opposite tack and try to make it clear that they're doing the recipient a favor by messaging them.

(And then there're the people who skip the foreplay and go straight for asking for phone numbers, Snapchat, Skype names or just nude pics.)

The problem with *any* of these approaches[6] is the assumption that you can dictate or influence the other person's actions. Not only is it impossible, but it's not the *point* of sending a message. The point of messaging someone on a dating site is very simple: you're trying to connect with someone and start a conversation.

There are three components to a good first message:

1. **It's Short:** If you're writing more than a paragraph, then you're writing too much; not only is sending somebody a novella not more likely to make them respond, but it means you're expending too much time on each person you message. That's going to exhaust you and you'll end up emotionally overinvesting in every person you try to contact. That's a great way to shred your self-esteem, especially if you're sending that message to a cold account.

2. **It's Simple:** You're not trying to be Shakespeare. You're not sending love poetry. You're trying to start a conversation. Stick to the obvious: what is it about their profile that caught your attention. What do you find interesting about them? What, based on their profile, do you have in common? Ask a question or two about their interests. Make it about *them*. You don't need to include crazy amounts of information about yourself; that's what your profile is for. If they're

curious about you, they'll either check you out or have seen your profile already.

3. **It's Heartfelt:** Authenticity is the gold standard of online dating. Being disingenuous or fake, whether you're trying to present a false front or just saying what you think they want to hear, is just going to trip you up. It makes it impossible to connect with people and that will screw you over. It's better to be genuine and honest, even if what you're looking for is a one-night stand. You're more likely to find people who're looking for the same thing as you if you aren't wasting time trying to trick or ease people into things.

Take time to proof-read your message, sign it with your name and hit send. And then... forget about it. There's nothing you can do to make your letter work better or faster. Avoid the temptation to use read receipts or other services; all this will do is increase any anxiety you may have about how your message is received. Either it will work and they will respond, or they won't. Getting hung up on how many responses you get or how quickly people reply to you will only make you more anxious and leave you giving that person far more significance than they deserve. Fire and forget and move on to the next person you're interested in.

Working From A Template

Online dating is a numbers game. If you're going to be proactive and make the first move, you're going to need to send a lot of emails. Spending all of your time trying to get that *one* person to go out with you is counterproductive just from an efficiency standpoint, never mind an emotional one. That person may be great, but there are plenty of others out there who are equally as wonderful. You should be messaging *many* women who interest you.

Of course, when you're sending out all those emails, it can be incredibly time-consuming to craft a new and unique message to each and every person. It can be incredibly tempting to want to cut down on the initial time investment by writing some all-purpose material that works on everybody you might want to get in touch with. Wouldn't that be falling in line with the philosophy of minimal investment for maximum returns?

Well… no. In fact, it's going to make things *worse. M*ost of the women you'll run into on dating sites are already wise to that trick; many, *many* men send very blatant copy-paste messages that make it clear that they've never read their profiles. To be perfectly blunt: when you send dating form letters, you're implying that you couldn't be bothered to actually try to connect with them and insulting their intelligence for good measure. All this does is tell her that you're shotgunning as many messages as possible and really don't care who responds.

Now that having been said: if you're going to be sending out messages, you're going to want to streamline things. If we go back to the 80/20 rule, your messages aren't in the 20% of the effort that gets the result; your *profile* is. Your message is to start the conversation. Period. Spending more time than is necessary on the message is wasteful.

So how do you message people in an efficient manner without spamming the same email over and over again? You work from a template.

A template is different from a form letter; where a form letter is exactly the same every time, a template provides you a structure to work from, streamlining your process while making each letter unique. Every first-contact email has certain beats that you want to hit: who you are, why you're interested in her, what commonalities you share and a little bait to prompt her to respond. You can change and update a template's structure as needed, but every message still remains unique and specific to the person you're contacting.

The structure is simplicity itself: a greeting, what it is about them from their profile that you like, a question to prompt a response, a little bit about you, and then "I hope to talk to you soon" and your name. Two or three lines for each section. Boom, done. Each section should showcase a your personality. Injecting a little friendly playfulness or even outright silliness can go a long way towards encouraging people to check you out.

Don't be afraid to write out the "about me" section in advance; it'll save you time in the long-run and it allows you to fine-tune it rather than hitting "send" and then kicking yourself because you realized you could've said something wittier.

So using that idea, a very randomized example would be:

"Hey, you seem like you're cool and I wanted to say 'hey.' So… hey! Your interest in skydiving caught my attention… I've been dying to try it, but I can't convince my friends to come jump out of a perfectly good airplane with me. The closest I've come is parasailing and the occasional roller-coaster. I love that moment right before free-fall when everything's just so intense and the tension builds up, you know?

A little about me: I'm a librarian with awesome tattoos and a dark mysterious past, involving sinister monks, ancient manuscripts and tension-filled pursuit through the back streets of Florence. It's a long story. :P

Like I said: you seem like you're a really interesting person and I'd love to get to know you. Hope to talk to you soon,

Gerald"

You'll want to adapt your template to the site. OKCupid, for example, will open a chat window when you message someone who's online; in those cases, you'll want to treat it as though you were texting someone for the first time. Some sites treat messages as actual emails, with subject lines while others just display the first line of the message. If you have the option of including a subject, use something offbeat instead of the usual "hey" or "greetings"; I've always had success with "Pirates are inherently cooler than ninjas."

It can take a little time to get into the rhythm of crafting the right first contact message. Even working from a template means that you'll be massaging and fine-tuning things as you go. But once you've gotten the hang of it, it will speed up your messages and let you reach out to people quickly, efficiently and effectively.

WHAT ABOUT CHATS AND INSTANT MESSAGES?

Some dating sites offer the ability to instant message people who happen to be online at the same time you are, rather than sending a message. As a general rule, I advise against doing this. Having a chat window pop up without warning can be jarring and feel a little invasive. Obviously, this is *not* a feeling you want to inspire in people you're hoping to meet. Worse, if you haven't had any contact before, then you get to enjoy all of the fun of the stilted and uncomfortable small-talk of a networking event without the benefit of snacks and booze.

The obvious exception are sites and apps that are specifically built around texting and instant messaging, such as Tinder and Grindr. In those cases, the ability to text back and forth is predicated on mutual interest and you *expect* to hear from them when there's a match. When you start chatting with somebody on a dating site, you want to get the conversation rolling immediately. The polite preliminaries - the exchanges of "Hi", "Hey", "How're you?" "Not bad, you?" and so forth - are boring and just leave you both feeling awkward. Instead, it's better in the long run to engage with them and start getting to know each other instead of awkwardly playing conversational volleyball. You're better off to lead with a question or observation. What you say ultimately depends on your personality - speaking for myself, I'm a little more forward, so I'm more likely to lead with something absurd like "Zombies are inherently scarier than ghosts, true or false?"

What you *don't* want to do is comment on their looks, their bodies or to start hitting on them. Even on dedicated hook-up apps, it's rude, off-putting and betrays low social intelligence. Just because someone's specifically looking for casual sex doesn't mean that all you have to do is show up and assume everything's good to go. You need to build those connections and work on compatibility and chemistry. Similarly: no unsolicited pictures of your junk. If they didn't ask *specifically*, then they don't want to see it and you're just being an asshole.

Other conversational no-nos include asking the same ten questions everyone *always* asks when getting to know people: who are you, what do you do, where did you grow up, where did you go to school, etc. Skip the biography and get to more interesting questions that let you *really* get to know them. Don't be overly serious: you should be having fun batting questions back and forth. "Who's your favorite James Bond? What about your favorite Bond Girl?" "What podcasts do you listen to?" "What's your biggest musical guilty pleasure?" "*Game of Thrones* or *House of Cards?*" "*Arrow* or *Daredevil?*"

Spend a little time warming up with questions like these before getting to deeper topics; you'll both feel more at ease with one another instead of sitting there and cringing awkwardly at each "not much... what's up with you?"

A general rule of thumb when it comes to chatting and small talk: Interesting or controversial beats "pleasant" every time. You don't want to be rude or combative, but talking about polarizing subjects, including religion and politics, is far more enjoyable than sticking to "safe" topics like whether they have siblings or what movies they've seen recently.

---

[1] This comes from OKCupid co-founder Christian Rudder. Women, by comparison, have a 40% chance of receiving a response when they cold-email a man.

[2] But not all; Zoosk still uses credits and micro-transactions as *well* as a subscription fee.

[3] Most of the time, anyway. One of the perks of OKCupid's A-list subscriptions is that you can see who's

rated or liked you.

[4] Negging: a left-handed compliment or sarcastic insult intended to demonstrate that you're socially superior to her and therefor she should be seeking your approval. Thought to bring down "bitch shields". Doesn't actually work and generally makes you look like an asshole.

[5] Compliance tests mean you're trying to make the other person jump through hoops to demonstrate their interest. The larger the hoop they're willing to jump through, the more committed and interested they are. The theory is that the more you can get someone to do what you ask, the more they'll continue to do so. It's akin to the "Yes Ladder" in high-pressure sales - the more you get someone to say "yes", the more they'll continue to say "yes" until you get what you want.

[6] Aside from obvious issues like being glaringly rude...

Six

TAKING IT OFFLINE

SETTING UP THE FIRST DATE

People get oddly hung up on making the transition from talking online to meeting in public. The point of online dating is *dating* after all; if you like someone well enough online, it's only natural to want to meet up to see whether that chemistry continues in person. The biggest mistake that people make is assuming that showing interest is somehow bad; it ties into the idea that "whomever cares the least, has the most power". This is a lovely thought if you treat every relationship as a contest for dominance, less so for a kindling a happy romance.

As a general rule of thumb, if you've exchanged three or more solid messages or long, interesting chats with plenty of back and forth, then it's worth asking the person to meet up. You don't need to make a big production out of asking for a date - in fact, doing so tends to seem a little overboard. You're better off making an low-key invitation: something along the lines of "Hey, I've been really enjoying talking to you and I'd like to continue this. Maybe over coffee?" is sufficient.

Your match may not be ready quite yet; that's fine. Some people will want to talk a little bit more before they're ready to take it offline. The important part is putting meeting up in person on the table. The longer you take to "work up the courage" to ask or "to get comfortable with them", the less likely you're going to meet at all. The more you message back and forth *without* asking them out, the less interested you'll look. It doesn't matter if you're both waiting for the other person to make the first move; if everybody's waiting, nobody's dating.

The other thing to keep in mind: once you've asked, *leave it alone*. The ball's in their court now. Badgering them repeatedly will only make them decide they'd rather *not* go out with you. If you've asked someone to meet and they don't give any suggestions about times that might work better for *them*, then you're better off simply meeting up with someone else. You've shown that you're interested. If they're interested in meeting, they'll respond to your invitation or propose another date and time.

THE PRE-DATE DATE

The one universal fear that men and women have[1] when it comes to online dating is very simple: their date's going to be boring. Dates that are absolute disasters at least have the potential to be entertaining stories later on. On the other hand, dates that drag on and on, leaving you mourning the two hours of your life (and price of drinks) that you will never get back will murder parts of your soul with teeny-tiny knives.

Chemistry you have online doesn't always transfer to chemistry in person, which is why meeting up is important. However, at the same time, you don't want to devote an entire evening to meeting someone who may very well bore you to tears. Even if you cut out early with a pre-arranged excuse, you've still spent time getting ready and heading to the bar or restaurant; that's time you could've used on Netflix after all. This is why you should consider the pre-date date.

The pre-date date is very simple: it is a low-key, low-investment, time-limited get-together to feel each other out. It is, for all intents and purposes an audition; you're gauging how much you like this person in the flesh, whether they're as cool in person as they are online, whether they seem like they're likely to viciously murder you and wear your skin as a flesh-suit.

The best pre-date date locations are coffeehouses. Unlike bars or restaurants, they encourage a relaxed, lounging atmosphere and, critically, are quiet enough to allow for conversation without shouting over the music. The food and drink options are inexpensive and simple and there isn't the same pressure to eat and get out, nor do you have a server coming by every fifteen minutes and interrupting the conversation. Even better: many coffeehouses offer boardgames, which make for excellent first date activities. A pre-date date is designed to be flexible. Propose an artificial time-limit - usually around 30 minutes to an hour, relatively early in the day. Not only does this minimize the amount of time wasted if the date is a dud, but you have an automatic, no-questions asked eject button; you've simply got a thing to do afterwards. In an absolute worst case scenario, you've had a cup of coffee or two and played a game of Scrabble - hardly a massive imposition on your time or finances.

At the same time, however, if things are going well and the two of you are clicking, then you're in a perfect position to keep the date going. This is where a little preparation goes a long way. If at all possible, you want to choose a coffeehouse that's within walking distance to other bars or restaurants or points of interest. If you've decided to continue the date, then it's much easier to propose going down the street to get an early dinner, visit a nearby wine bar or take a walk in the park than it is to coordinate driving to another venue. The walk is better for generating chemistry and keeping the momentum going - anything that elevates your heart-rate, even slightly, is going to make you feel more aroused and connected to one another. Plus: you can't keep the conversation going if you're driving in separate cars.

Regardless of whether you cut things off at the half-hour mark, or you talk well into the night, if you've made it through the pre-date date, then you can propose a "real" date next time. You want to avoid the obvious - and *boring* - standards of "dinner and a movie"; not only has everybody done this date to death, but you're ensuring that the two of you won't be talking or interacting for at least two hours. This is a terrible idea in the early stages of dating - you're still very much in the "getting to know you" phase of things. Two hours of silence is two hours you could have spent talking, teasing and flirting with one another.

Instead, you want to plan a date that allows you to interact with one another. As a general rule of thumb, active dates beat ones where you're sitting around and exciting dates beat pleasant ones. If you're looking for interesting and original date ideas, I have a number of them over on Paging Dr. NerdLove. Taking your date to a sushi-making class will be far more enjoyable and memorable than the last five people who took her to a bar.

GETTING THAT SECOND DATE

Whether you have a pre-date date or launch straight into a full date right off the jump, there's one constant in online dating: getting the first date is easy; the *second* dates tend to be rarer. The key to getting a second date is very simple: you ace the first.

People have an unfortunate tendency of shooting themselves in the foot on first dates. They may be perfectly lovely and charming under most circumstances, but it's the *little* things that add up quickly to "I don't want to see this person again."

Now, I go into more detail about what makes a killer first date and how to make sure you get a second in *New Game+*[2], but we're going to cover a few of the basics here. So in order to avoid turning a great first date into an unpleasant memory, remember:

Pay Attention

Your date is about the *two* of you - not you and your date and your phone or you, your date and the TV. I shouldn't need to mention this, but I have lost track at how many people I've seen blow an otherwise wonderful date by paying more attention to their phone than the person sitting across from them. Pulling your phone out and leaving it on the table - yes, people do this on dates - is the height of rudeness; it tells your date that any potential messages are more important than they are. Leave your phone in your pocket where it belongs. If you *absolutely* need to check your phone - and it better be for something more dire than checking your fantasy draft's stats - slip off to the bathroom first. Otherwise there's nothing you need to see that won't wait until after you've said goodnight.

Give your *full* attention to your date. One of the keys to charisma is making someone feel like they're most fascinating person on Earth. You can't do that if your eyes are flicking to the TV behind her.

Ask Questions

Everybody underestimates the power of a good conversationalist. Someone who knows how to master the art of conversation is *always* in demand; they are the ones who make you feel as if you've known them for *years*. They're easy to talk to and leave you feeling as though you could tell them *anything*. Their secret is deceptively uncomplicated: they ask questions. More specifically, they ask the *right* questions. Now is the time when you want to get to know your date, so ask them about themselves. What are they passionate about? What did they want to be when they grew up? What was their favorite movie as a child? What band do they absolutely *refuse* to admit they like publicly? Listen to their answers, find some way of relating to it ("Woah, you loved *The Watcher In the Woods?* I didn't know anyone else saw that!") and then use their answer as a springboard for a follow-up.

Most people don't listen; they just wait for their turn to talk. There are few things more irritating than someone who asks a question and then immediately launches into a lecture without even stopping to hear what the other person has to say. By asking questions and showing that you care about her answers, you're showing her that you're interested. And interested is *interesting*.

Trust me: you want to be interesting.

Relax

I can't emphasize this one enough: calm down. Take a deep breath, hold it, then release it slowly. It's understandable that you'd be nervous. You've worked hard to get to this point and you want everything to go perfectly. You want her to like you but you don't want to come across like you're desperate for her to like you, you're hoping that you'll get her to go back to your place or at least get a good night kiss out of things and what if you say something wrong or, or…

Chill.

There's not nearly as much to worry about as you think. The last thing you want to do is be so wound up that you can't possibly enjoy the date. Believe me: your date wants this to be as successful as you do; *nobody* goes on dates looking for reasons to ditch somebody. Worry less about trying to impress your date and focus more about trying to *connect* with them. By taking a few deep breaths, soothing those jangled nerves and loosening those clenched muscles, you'll have a better time… and have a better chance of getting that second date.

Make it Clear You Want To See Her Again

You've made it this far. Now it's time to stick the landing. At the end of the date, if you've had a good time, then you want to open up the possibility of another. There's no profit in soft-selling things or doing the "well, maybe, if you're free…" hesitation dance. Say it straight-forward: "I've had a great time, and I'd really like to see you again." It's short, simple and displays confidence. Don't worry about proposing another date right then and there; unless you have an activity you were *already* planning on that you want to invite her to, then there will likely be a bit of schedule checking before anyone can say for sure. Just put it out there and let her meet you half-way.

And a word of advice: *don't* badger her twice a day every day to set up that next date; if she wants to see you again, she *will*. Getting insecure, needy or demanding is a *great* way to snatch defeat from the jaws of victory.

---

[1] Individually, it differs. Men worry that women aren't going to look like their photos. Women worry that men are going to murder them.

[2] Available August 11, from Thought Catalog!

SEVEN

GET OUT OF THE OFFLINE DATING MINDSET

GET OUT OF THE OFFLINE DATING MINDSET

One of the things that nobody tells you about online dating is that it's entirely different from meeting people in person. On the surface, this seems fairly obvious - you're swiping and texting and browsing profiles, not trying to approach strangers at a bar or trying to transition from awkward small-talk to flirting with a friend of a friend at a house party. In some ways it feels like an unholy combination of posting on Facebook and ordering a pizza. But while some aspects transfer completely between online and offline dating - conversation is essentially the same, regardless of whether you're on Kik or talking in person - there's still a considerable difference between the two. One of the reasons people get so frustrated with online dating is that they never get out of the offline dating mindset.

For 99.99999% of human history, all of our interpersonal relationships - whether platonic or romantic - have been carried out face to face. Everything about how we interact with others, both mechanically and socially is predicated on being able to actually *see* them, touch them and smell them. It's literally hard-coded in our brains. Even when our communication networks developed and expanded - through the invention of language, then writing, then telegraphs, telephones and computer networks - our personal relationships were conducted face to face. No matter how much the rules and rituals of courtship changed over the millennia, they were all based on our interacting in person.

Now that we live our entire lives on the Internet, those rules have gone out the window... but we still try to treat this new way of interacting as though it were exactly the same as interacting in person and we get angry and frustrated when it doesn't work out.

To make the most of online dating, you have to shed the offline dating mindset. You have to recognize that the way we form relationships with people online is fundamentally different from the way we do in person.

COMMUNICATION IS KEY

One of the first things you have to recognize when it comes to online dating is that we've paradoxically made communicating *harder*. Sure, we're able to converse with people around the world in real time, sending insanely complex information across networks faster than the speed of thought... but in doing so, we've severely limited our ability to be understood. And I don't just mean trying to translate chan-speak, Twitter shorthand, Tumblrisms, greentext[1], slang terms and memes without resorting to UrbanDictionary.

Studies show that between 75% and 93% of communication is entirely non-verbal. When we meet somebody in person, we communicate through eye contact, and gesture, through our posture and our facial expressions, even through the way we array ourselves when we're standing perfectly still. When we are talking to one another, we have hundreds of verbal and non-verbal cues and ticks that carry volumes of information and can completely change the context of what's being said. It's not just what you say but how you're saying it. When you say the words "I hate you" to somebody, the tone of your voice and the expression on your face all affect how the other person interprets the meaning. Pitch your voice lower and glare at them and you're telling them that you hate them. Growl it with a Texas accent and you're imitating Yosemite Sam. Say it with an upwards inflection and a punch in the shoulder and you're making a joke.

When you communicate through text - whether through email, chat, direct messages or even hand-written letters, all of that extra information *goes away*. You're left trying to determine meaning through context and what you assume you know about the other person's personality. Tone does not carry through text. It is incredibly easy to mistake joking or sarcastic statements as being meant seriously. Even literally symbolic gestures meant to emulate facial expressions like emoji and emoticons can't capture the same level of nuance and meaning; in fact it can makes things *worse*.[2] Plus: they're seen as childish and immature.

Communicating online means that you need to be as clear and understandable as possible. Anything that you say that can be misinterpreted almost certainly *will*. When it comes to online dating, you're messaging total strangers. They don't have any frame of reference for your personality that would allow them to make an educated guess as to whether you're being sarcastic or completely serious. This is why sexually charged flirting, references to body parts or similar behavior is a bad idea while you're messaging each other back and forth: they can't tell when you're joking and you can't tell when their joking deflections mean that they are playing along or uncomfortably chuckling and hoping that you'll catch the hint and change the subject. Similarly, that ironic joke about sluts or being a nice guy? Absent any other indicators, they're going to take you at your word.

This goes double for pick-up artist routines and gimmicks; "cocky-funny" jokes and negs just make you sound like an asshole and "hah ha, that was a joke just kidding" has never gotten somebody laid.

This doesn't mean that you can't be funny or silly in your interactions with people... but you have to recognize the potential to be misunderstood is incredibly high. If you're not good at conveying humor through text, then you're better off saving the jokes for when you trade phone numbers or meet in person.

SHOW, DON'T TELL

Understanding the differences between online and offline communication is also part of how you make the most out of your profile. Many of the people who have trouble making online dating work for them make the cardinal mistake that gets drilled into anyone who's ever taken a basic creative writing course: they're too busy *telling* about themselves instead of showing. Some of the oldest and most boring cliches of online dating are the people who just say that they have some attractive quality... without anything to back it up. Saying that you're funny or spontaneous or romantic is the dating site equivalent of "I listen to a little bit of everything except country and rap." It's so generic as to mean nothing. Everyone has heard it a thousand times *before* they saw your profile and they didn't believe it any of those times either.

Talk is cheap. Anybody can say *anything* about themselves. *Demonstrating* these qualities is what's important. You could very well be telling the complete and unvarnished truth, but if your profile doesn't reflect it, people are less likely to believe you. You may well have won a Pulitzer, but if your self summary is full of typos, grammatical errors and choppy, inelegant sentences, everyone will call bullshit on you.

In the great chain of credibility, telling

something is the least believable. Having a second party vouch for you is more believable, but being able to show that quality is instant credibility.

For example: I could tell people that I'm Dr. NerdLove, millionaire, and that I own a mansion and a yacht. Most folks would nod their heads and go about their business secure in their belief that I am completely full of shit.

On the other hand, if someone's friend tells them about the incredibly lavish party they went to at stately NerdLove Manor last weekend, then that person would be more inclined to believe that yes, I am indeed a millionaire with a mansion and a yacht. And if I happen to sail past that person's house – which is quite the feat when you live in the middle of a land-locked city, let me tell you – then they'll definitely believe it.

This is why you want to *demonstrate* those qualities, to the best of your ability. And since you're dealing with dating profiles, that means using your words and your pictures.

Take humor for example. Everyone claims to be funny in their profile and most of them are as dull as dry toast when you meet them in person. If you want people to believe that you're a laugh riot, you have to prove it. If you have a sharp wit or a way with words, then find a place in your profile to make people laugh. Don't call attention to it, just work it in there; your "About Me" section or "What I'm Looking For" are great places to show it. If your brand of humor trends to the physical or being silly, then post that picture of you as the Stay-Puft Marshmallow Man from last Halloween or that time you posed with a statue as though you were part of the scenery.

Being specific works better than giving generalities. Telling somebody you're adventurous or that you love to travel is relatively generic. Talking about your recent trip to Ankor Wat is better. Having a photo of you in front of Ta Prohm is better still. Don't say that you're athletic, mention that you take part in an amateur soccer league or have a cool photo of you and some of your teammates after your latest scrimmage.

Yes, I'm giving a lot of priority to photos. Remember: the web is a visual medium and it's unofficial motto is "pics or it didn't happen."

Photos that back up what you say in your profile will give you more appeal – and credibility – than just saying something.

Don't Get Hung Up On One Person

Another example of the offline dating mindset that gets people in trouble is that they narrow their focus too early.

Many people, especially when they're getting into online dating for the first time, tend to treat online dating as though they were talking to somebody in a bar. In the physical world, you only flirt with one person at a time; if you strike out with that person, then you move on to the next person. Unless you're Hank Moody, Barney Stintson and Captain Jack Harkness[3] combined, flirting with several different people simultaneously is a major faux-pas[4] and likely to leave you going home alone – possibly wearing several drinks. We often carry this mindset over into online dating and start to give one person – usually the first one to respond – all of our attention, ignoring everybody else until that first conversation has run its course. Even the more proactive searchers will carry on only one conversation at a time; they may be shotgunning messages into every profile that catches their eye, but they stop as soon as they get their first response.

This is a mistake – and one that makes online dating considerably more inefficient and tedious. When you focus on only one person at a time, you're choosing to give up the advantages of online dating. The rules and etiquette of online and offline interaction are different. When you're talking to people in person, it's virtually impossible to hold several separate conversations simultaneously. The human brain simply doesn't have the bandwidth to give everybody your full and undivided attention. Because you're communicating online, you are capable of carrying on several asynchronous conversations at the same time - chatting with persons X and Y while also sending out an introductory message to person Z. You can and *should* cast your net far and wide. Even for dedicated monogamists and people who are looking for long-term relationships, focusing on one single person over-invests them with too much importance and leaves you open to needless grief.

There are many, *many* false starts when it comes to online dating and people *you* like won't necessarily like you back or be as interested in you as you are in them. When you start to focus on one person to the exclusion of all others and invest in them emotionally before you even *meet,* never mind start a relationship with them, then it's going to hurt that much more when they don't like you back.

Which brings us to the other reason why talking to one person at a time is a mistake: *you* aren't the only person *they're* talking to. Remember how I said that you can carry on multiple conversations at once? Other people are doing that as well. The odds are good that the person who caught your eye has caught other people's eye - or that they may be actively messaging other people that *they* are interested in. As cold as this sounds, there's no real reason for them to ignore everybody else just to talk to you. You're a relative stranger to them, and they're gauging whether you're worth their time.

Yes, this seems rude… but that's because it's happening to *you.* Think of how many people *you* shrug off because you're not interested in *them.* I guarantee you: there will be people who message you who you will decide aren't worth it. People will lose interest in talking to you, even when you think things are going well. You will lose interest in *them* too. Conversations and flirtations will end up going nowhere and fade into nothingness. That's part and parcel of how online dating works. The more you spread your attention out, the more successful you will be - and the less the near-misses and fades will affect you.

Speaking of which:

PLAY THE NUMBERS

At its core, dating is a numbers game. No matter who you are, you're going to have to date a number of people before you find someone who you're compatible with. Nobody is so lucky that they find their perfect match with the very first person they ever date. You have to go through multiple first dates before you find someone to be in your first serious relationship with. Unless you're part of a *very* small minority, then you're more than likely going to go through multiple relationships in your lifetime.

That's part of how dating works… and this applies to online dating as well.

One of the great intellectual fallacies we all suffer from is the idea that we're perfectly conscious of what we like and why. We like to assume that we know exactly who we're attracted to and what it is that draws us to them. In reality, however, much of what makes us interested in people occurs without our conscious knowledge.

The human brain is a wonder of information gathering and processing; we take in seemingly disparate data, sort through it, compare it and draw conclusions from it almost instantaneously. When we see somebody, we are absorbing a plethora of minute details that give us an intuitive grasp of who they are and how we feel about them long before we go up and introduce ourselves. Everything from how they stand to how they talk, who they talk to, how they act around their friends, how they smell, even the pitch and timbre of their voice inform us as to whether we're attracted enough to them that we would want to make that first approach. We process *all* of these signals so rapidly that we're often unaware of it; to our conscious mind, we're just eliding over the ones who we read as "nope, not interested" while we narrow our focus on the people who do it for us.

All of this subconscious presentation and filtering is lost in online dating. Just as we can't use vocal tonality to give context via text, we're unable to pick up on these little clues and micro-signals when we read somebody's dating profile. All we have are our words and our photos, so we have to consider how to craft as attractive a snapshot of ourselves as possible. We're left to divine as much of that information as possible from the clues that we *do* have: their dating profile and the messages we share.

But even when we find ourselves intrigued or attracted by somebody we've met on a dating site, there is no guarantee that this will translate to an attraction in person. We can talk all we want about the beauty and purity of somebody's mind and soul and getting to know them without presumptions based on looks, but we're physical beings. Our meat-sacks are as responsible for attraction as our brains. All of the intellectual compatibility in the world doesn't guarantee that you're going to want to hook up with them in person. Maybe they have a habit that turns you off. Maybe they're rude to the waiter. Maybe they're a lousy kisser. Or it could be some indescribable quality that you may not be able to name but simply isn't there, no matter how much you wish it were.

Being perfect for you on paper doesn't mean much when there's something about the other person that simply doesn't ring your bell.

There are going to be dates that don't go anywhere. There will be people who seem great online who you won't click with in person. You're going to have false positives and near misses. This is true for *everyone*, no matter who they are. It's part of the price of entry, and it's better to adjust your expectations accordingly instead of dealing with the slow burn of "WHY WON'T THE MAGICAL BOX PROVIDE ME WITH PERFECT SEX RIGHT NOW?"

That doesn't mean that it won't be *fun*, mind you. Yeah, you will meet people who will leave you feeling like your time would be better spent watching grass grow, but you'll *also* meet people who may not be right but who are a lot of fun. You'll have dates that are only good for stories. You'll have dates that don't go anywhere but are fun in and of themselves. And as you go through these, you'll get better at finding the people who you *are* compatible with and who you will have amazing times with.

You just have to be willing to invest the time.

You have to play the numbers.

He Who Hesitates Is Lost

The number one complaint I get from guys who're frustrated with online dating comes from people who pull the "fade-away". At first, everything seems to be going well! They messaged somebody, that person wrote them back. The conversations starts strong - they're practically writing novellas to each other. But over the course of a week or two, something seems to change. Those replies start to get shorter and shorter, until he's just getting one or two sentences back, if you get anything beyond a "lol" or "heh". And then... radio silence. A day goes by. Then two. Then a week. Nothing. He knows they've logged into their account - he's not proud, but he's been checking to see when their most recent activity was. But they never hear back.

Now he's left wondering just what the hell happened and whether or not he should try to message them again.[5]

Nine times out of ten when this happens, it's been because the guy took too long to get to the point. They get so caught up in trying to impress their digital coquette that they forget to, y'know, actually ask them on a date.

(The remaining one time out of ten is that the other person thought the guy was nice enough, but they decided they wanted to date someone else.)

Look: I get it. I can understand wanting to make sure there's some chemistry there or doing your due diligence to make sure the other person's not an axe-murderer. I can understand not wanting to seem too eager or desperate. I can understand that you don't want to risk rejection by asking her out before you're absolutely, positively, 100% sure that she'll say "yes."But the cold hard truth of the matter is that the longer you take to getting around to actually *asking her out*, the more likely that either a) she's going to assume you're not interested and move on or b) somebody else is going to ask her out first. Remember: you're most likely *not* the only person she's talking to[6]. Don't get me wrong: this doesn't mean you're in a race with every other guy out there. It simply means that people aren't going to wait for you forever to summon up the courage to ask them to meet up. No matter how nifty she thinks you may be, if you're never taking any concrete steps to move things to the next level, then she has no real reason *not* to take someone else up on their offer.

Yes, she could ask *you* out. But you can't just rely on other people doing the work for you. You're going to have to be willing to be proactive here. It's called online dating, not online pen-pal-ing. The point of online dating is to *date*.

The longer your conversation goes on, the more emotional momentum you're bleeding and the greater the likelihood that you're never going to actually see them in person. If you've had three to four quality emails back and forth, you should be trying to set up a date. Constantly swapping messages back and forth gets you nowhere and ultimately just wastes your time and leaves you frustrated and alone. An interim step like talking on the phone or texting or instant-messaging just delays things further; there's nothing that texting you directly is going to tell them that they wouldn't get from a messaging site. Exchanging numbers makes sense when you've set up a date - you want to be able to get in touch with each other in case things change before your date without having to log back in to the dating site. But as a step between messaging and meeting, it's a time waster.

You like them. They like you. You've got some intellectual and emotional chemistry. Now it's time to find out if you have any *physical* chemistry.

Ask them out already.

---

[1] See what I mean? Odds are good at least *some* of that sounds like gibberish to you and leaves you feeling *old as hell*.

[2] Volumes have been written about the people who think that adding :p or ;) at the end of a mean text or tweet means the recipient shouldn't take offense.

³ Aka John Barrowman's pansexual and utterly shameless character in Doctor Who and Torchwood. Google him. And then read my posts about him at doctornerdlove.com

⁴ The other exception, of course, is if you're starring in an episode of *The Bachelor*.

⁵ Spoiler alert: no. No he should *not*.

⁶ And *she* should not be the only person *you* are talking to…

Eight

WHY WOMEN DON'T RESPOND... AND WHAT TO DO ABOUT IT.
DON'T RUIN YOUR CHANCES BEFORE YOU EVEN START.

One of the things that will make a difference in your dating success is very simple: learn from other people's mistakes so you don't make your *own*. And there's no better way to learn about other people's mistakes than to see them yourself.

In 2014, a Reddit user wrote in the TwoXChromosomes subreddit about his experiences posing as a woman on OKCupid. OKCThrowaway22221 wanted to prove something that many people commonly accept as fact: that women have it easier in online dating. So he created an account, filled out the profile, picked a suitably attractive photo for his new persona and waited for the messages to roll in.

And boy howdy *did* they. Within 20 minutes, he had four ongoing conversations, with more and more messages coming in. And then things started getting uncomfortable. One of the people he was talking to suddenly started trying to steer the conversation towards sex, despite OKCThrowaway22221 telling him to stop. Another started demanding "her" phone number and insisting that he'd treat her right. Then there were the people demanding that "she" cam with them. Or who wanted to know if she would meet up with them within the hour. Or who sent dick pics. There were the ones who got pissed off and aggressive when "she" would say she wasn't into no-strings-attached sex.

OKCThrowaway22221 lasted *less than two hours* before he got so uncomfortable that he deleted the profile entirely.

I'd had a similar experience. My friend Emma had just broken up with her boyfriend and wanted to reactivate her OKCupid account. She was hoping that I might be able to help her fine-tune things so that she could start dating again. The emails started rolling in almost as soon as she'd clicked "confirm", which meant that I had a prime opportunity to see some of the winners who were messaging her. There's nothing like seeing "Can I cum on your tits?"[1] as the first line on an email from a complete stranger to remind you that maybe online dating isn't the cornucopia for women that a lot of people think it is.

Being able to experience online dating from a woman's perspective – if at one step removed – is something of an eye-opener to just how many guys seem determined to make sex vanish into thin air. For every guy who complains about the number of emails he sends into the void with no response, there are ten women who're getting two dozen from dudes who make their skin crawl… and ironically, it would be so easy to stand out from the pack.

YOU DIDN'T ACTUALLY *READ* HER PROFILE

Remember when I said you had to make it clear that you actually *read* her profile when you contacted her? I didn't mean "just skim the damned thing and look for something you could plug into your introduction e-mail", I said *read* it.

Y'see, one valuable part of online dating is that it lets you pre-screen your potential dates. You can look for matching goals in life, you can look for similar interests or even just filter by the fact that you like six-foot tall Amazons with tattoos and shaved heads.

It also lets you screen for potential deal-breakers - both yours and *hers*. And many women will helpfully tell you in advance what their deal breakers are. If she declares that she only wants to date Christian men who own corgis and drive Smart Cars and you don't match *any* of those categories, you really have no room to complain when she tosses your message in the trash without even reading it.

"But women shouldn't pre-judge me based on an arbitrary standard!" I hear you cry. "I'm a special little snowflake! Surely I'm awesome enough that she can overlook whatever strange objections she might normally have in me!" And then I start laughing and reaching for my bottle of Jefferson's Reserve.

Yes, many people's stated deal breakers are arbitrary from an outsider's perspective. It may seem needlessly picky to you. That's fine. But she has the right to set her standards wherever and however she likes. Our love-lives aren't a democracy. What we decide we do and don't want in a partner isn't up for a public vote. Complaining about it - *especially to them* - isn't going to make them suddenly realize they're being unfair and you should be given a shot. It only makes you look like a whiney asshole and nobody got ever got laid by debating the other person into bed.

If you aren't her desired height, income level, educational level or are slightly older than her stated preferences, you certainly can take your chances by throwing your hat in the ring anyway. Who knows: maybe you'll be so damn charming that you can actually overcome the little pet-peeves she has that would otherwise keep her from being interested in dating you. But sometimes she lists those deal-breakers for a good damn *reason*. She doesn't like dogs because she's allergic. She has health issues which means she has to stick to a specific diet and exposure to other types of food might kill her. She doesn't like smokers because she has a history of lung-cancer in her family. The list goes on and on.

Some people may be willing to overlook a deal-breaker or two. Most will not, and all you've ended up doing is wasting her time and yours when you could have been moving on to someone more receptive. If you think someone is too picky or insists on making people jump through too many hoops for your taste, *don't email them*.

Harris O'Malley

You Have A List of Demands...

One of the great things about online dating is how it lets you be as selective as you could possibly want when it comes to finding a prospective mate... no matter how outré or specific. Looking for a cosplay enthusiast? They're out there! Looking for your fursuit-sporting soulmate? More power to you. Don't want to date a smoker? You can filter them out. Looking for the lacto-ovo-pescatarian of your dreams? You can let people know that meat-eaters need not apply...

But – and there's always a but – there comes a point where your list of must-haves and unacceptable traits becomes a list of "this is why you're still single".

A while back, somebody posted what may well be the greatest Craigslist personals ad in history. It was glorious; not only did it include a list of prerequisites, demands and deal breakers that the individual had before he would even consent to write back to anyone who messaged him, it also included a 28 question FAQ just to make sure everybody was on the same page. He was an extreme example to be sure... but he's hardly the only one out there. Many guys are perfectly happy to insist that their prospective matches should jump through many hoops before they're allowed to communicate.

Take, for example, this segment of an introductory email that one NerdLove reader received from her online swain:

> I suppose you might be interested in what I look like. I do have pictures available to send, but for now let me tell you that I stand approx. 6'1" at about 220lbs. I have a broad / athletic build (like a linebacker, but with a neck *laughs*). Additionally, I am in the process of making several "self-improvements", including working on getting myself in the best shape of my life (learning to skate to play hockey, etc.). I had Lasik and no longer require glasses!! *BIG smiles* But I want to stress, I am doing these things for me, not to "make myself more attractive" *sincerely* I say that because the best part of me is one which cannot be seen in a picture.It is my heart.Incidentally, and this is also going to let me know if you actually read this *laughs*, if you respond to me and ask for a picture, I will cease correspondence with you. I realize that probably makes me seem like a big jerk, but you know, there are several reasons for my taking this approach. First, if somebody's focus is more on the physical then on my heart,

then she is not the girl for me. Looks are ever so fleeting. It doesn't matter if I look like a troll or prince charming. What matters should be my heart. Second, what I have found is that, for the most part, those people who simply respond with a request for pictures tend to be very young people, or people who are otherwise misrepresenting themselves, and "trolling" the internet for pictures. So, hopefully you will respect my position and agree that there is a better time to exchange pictures, after we are both more comfortable with each other *politely, sincerely*

(It's worth noting that this letter goes on for another two pages. *smiles* *politely*)

I'm going to be blunt here: you're not Brad Pitt. You're not Idris Elba, Ryan Gosling, Takeshi Kaneshiro, Kanye West, George Clooney, Michael B. Jordan, Zac Effron or any other gloriously handsome celebrity. You aren't so overwhelmed by female attention that the only way you can possibly handle the load is to filter out the unworthy with your list of Thou Shalt Nots and then demand that the remainder dance for your pleasure in order to earn your attention. Ditch the compliance ladder bullshit you picked up from a PUA forum and back away slowly. Same with any form of negging, or copy-pasted "demonstration of higher-value" tricks that you borrowed from Reddit's seduction boards. It doesn't work. Women who see this bullshit when they're checking you out will swipe left so quickly that their phones will leap out of their hands.

Look, I can appreciate the frustration that comes with hearing from people who you *know* aren't going to work out. It's understandable that maybe you just want to not waste time before finding out that the woman you've been flirting with believes in the Vagina Goblin who will bite off anything that enters her before she's been sanctified by the Holy Church. I'm not saying you can't have standards, or that you have to be willing to take on all comers. You're welcome to be as discerning as you want, as long as you realize that you're artificially restricting your potential dating pool… but when you've started outlining every single thing that you can't stand about women, you're telling people that you put the "mental" in judgmental.

RE: THAT DICK PIC YOU SENT ME

One of the great things about online dating is, when you're doing it right, it can make getting laid the easiest thing in the world. There are plenty of people online who are quite open to some no-strings attached nookie from the right guy, girl or various combinations thereof. I've messaged people on a Friday afternoon and ended back at their place by Saturday morning and set up a date with someone else for that evening.

Notice very carefully how I said "when you're doing it *right*." Most people *aren't*. In fact, the assholes out there are the ones making it harder for all the happy, horny men and women to hook up in peace.

Just because someone might be interested in casual sex – even if they flat out list "casual sex" in their "Looking For" field - doesn't mean that you can wave your dick at them[2] and expect them to get excited. Being open to a no-strings attached hook-up or wanting to find a friends-with-benefits relationship doesn't mean that they're interested in hearing about someone wanting to cum on their tits or that they want to talk about sex from the jump. The number of women who are willing to just leap into bed with somebody that they've never even met in person is so small as to be nonexistent. The risks are simply too high.

A woman who's interested in a casual hook-up wants to make sure that the sex is going to be *worth* it. Why should she bother taking the time to dress up and meet somebody for a drink and more if all that she's going to get out of it is 30 minutes of uncomfortable poking and prodding? She wants to feel some chemistry before she's going to take a chance… and even then, she's going to want to meet someplace neutral first to feel you out before you feel her *up*.

Seduction is a *dance*. There's a flow and a rhythm to it. It's flirting and teasing and increasing excitement and tension. It's something you build together, not something that you bludgeon into place. When you're trying to force the conversation to sex, you're coming off as the sketchy guy in the bar who keeps coming up to random women and asking for a handy in the bathroom. It's the *opposite* of attractive. It is the Anti-Sex Equation. The same goes for sending unsolicited dick pics. Sorry, but your cock isn't so impressive that people *need* to see it. That unasked-for, badly lit, awkwardly-angled shot of your wang isn't going to make someone's panties evaporate. If someone's interested in seeing Mr. Happy, they'll *ask*. And odds are, by that point, they'd rather see it in person anyway.

The secret to getting laid via OKCupid or another dating site is simple: go on dates. Build some chemistry. No, you may not be getting laid within the hour. You may not be having sex on the first date. But if you can show that you're a good guy, who's respectful *as well* as sexy? You'll be getting more sex than you know what to do with. Women are far more likely to sleep with somebody if they feel that the sex would be worth it... and the guy who's asking to tit-fuck her before he even says hello is demonstrating that no, it almost certainly *won't* be.

YOU ADVERTISE YOUR BITTERNESS

Attitude is a key part of success in dating. Not only does it color how you see the world, but how others perceive you; a positive outlook is far more attractive than someone sitting around, radiating anger and vitriol at everyone who passes by. There aren't any women sitting around thinking "You know what I really want? I'm looking for somebody who's favorite hobby is stewing in his own juices about how unfair the world is and how everybody sucks." Being a bitter, resentful mess just means that people will have better things to do than talk to you.

Something that every man needs to keep in mind when it comes to online dating – whether it's Tinder, OKCupid, Match, eHarmony, Plenty of Fish or any other dating site – is that every woman on there has inevitably received a message like this:

> Hey what u can look at my profile and can't say a simple hello, hold on lemme guess u have such an excessive profile description that I'm surprised u get any hits, anyway ur not hot enuff for this attitude reach up there pull ya tampon out ya stuck up bitch!

The Instagram account Bye Felipe, started and maintained by Alexandra Tweten, was created as an archive of the many, *many* repulsive and abusive messages that women get on sites like OKCupid and Tinder. There's also a plethora of blogs and Tumblrs like Ladies of OKCupid, WTFOKCreepy, OKCupidNiceGuys, Annals of Online Dating that document the awkward, ugly and flat out disgusting messages that women receive from would-be swains on a daily basis. And of course, there's the occasional unsolicited dick pic that shows up in their inboxes as well. There's only so much women can take before online dating fatigue kicks in or they get a sudden case of "FUCK THIS SHIT" before canceling their accounts altogether.

Clearly, this is something you would want to avoid.

So why in pluperfect hell would you broadcast

your shitty attitude to the world?

Let us say that you've been in contact with someone who seems perfect for you. She looks at your message and thinks "Hmm, cute photo, nice smile, funny message. Ok, I'm interested." And then she clicks on your profile to see this:

My Self Summary:
Hi! If you're reading this, then there's a 99.0009993% chance that I've messaged you. I try to stay positive but this site drags me down. Am I really that butt ugly?

Or perhaps:

You Should Message Me If:
…You want to, I suppose. If you're done dealing with all of those shirtless douchebags who'll treat you like shit and now that you've had your fun you're ready to come crawling to the nice guy you've been ignoring all this time.

In the span of three sentences, you've gone from being at the top of a *very* short list to convincing a potential match to board the Nope Train to FuckThisShitville. This is what we in the dating advice biz call "snatching defeat from the jaws of victory."

I can understand the impulse; online dating can be frustrating for everyone, men and women alike. There will be times when you want to vent your frustrations to the world… which is fine. Just do it offline. Negativity has no place in your online dating profile, especially when you're complaining about how undatable you are.

Plus: why would you want to even plant the idea that you're undatable in anybody's head in the first place?

If you have even the slightest suspicion that you come off as sullen and petulant, then you should have a friend you can trust to be bluntly honest with you look over your profile and help you edit out anything that even vaguely smacks of resentment and anger.

U Tlk Lik Thz.

As I said before: online dating is a text medium. 99% of your interactions on *any* dating site will be through text. You are attempting to woo and seduce women with your skill with language like poets of old, using nothing but beautiful letters and witty messages full of spark and meaning, conveying their passion through their mastery of the written language. Nobody has ever gotten laid with "u r SOO hawut".

Which is why I can't emphasize this enough: use complete sentences, correct spelling and *proper fucking grammar*. Tattoo this backwards on your forehead so you can see it every morning in the mirror. Shave your head if you need the room.

Using textspeak, SMS code, 1337sp33k, greentext or any other cutesy non-standard style of writing just makes you look like a goddamn idiot with a speech impediment to boot. Texting shorthand came about because of the inherent character limits in cellphone text-messaging services. Unless you're trying to pick women up via Twitter[3] you have all the time and space that you need to compose your reply. Typos are one thing; being completely illegible is another entirely.

This includes sending messages that consist entirely of "sup", "nm, u?" "Kik?" "Skype?" Brad Pitt isn't going to get laid by sending monosyllabic messages on Match and neither are you. Emojis aren't an acceptable substitute either.

Poor grammar and spelling are one of the top-ranked turn-offs for women online and it cripples your chances of hearing from anyone. For God's sake, every browser out there automatically highlights misspelled words. Sending a message full of misspellings, abbreviations and non-standard contractions is going to make you look you were too lazy to run the goddamned spellcheck before you hit "send".

Proper spelling and grammar. Proper spelling and *fucking* grammar.

It's A Zombie Profile

She's hot. She's single. She hasn't responded to a single email you ever sent… because you've been emailing a digital corpse. One of the risks (for suitably inflated values of "risk") that you're going to come across in the world of online dating is the dating site account that's dead yet still shuffling around: the zombie profile.

It looks for all the world like a normal account, but the person who owns it hasn't logged on in over three months… and probably never will. Sending messages, winks, pokes, flowers or other signs of interest is the digital equivalent to ringing the doorbell of an abandoned house. You're just wasting your time.

Zombie profiles litter every dating service – especially ones that rely on paid subscriptions. They may have let their subscription lapse, but never went through the procedure of actually removing their account – something that many dating sites make as difficult as possible in order to artificially inflate their numbers. They may have set up the profile on a lark and forgot about it after moving on when some other social network caught their attention. They may have started dating somebody they met on that very site and just never got around to closing their account or editing their profile to indicate that they're no longer on the market. Ultimately it doesn't matter: they're never going to respond to you, so you may as well quit worrying about 'em.

Start filtering for activity level in your searches. Most dating sites allow you to add "Active Within $TIME" to any search string. If the owner of the profile hasn't logged in within two weeks, the odds are good that you're looking at a zombie profile. Don't bother hoping that they'll notice the "You have a new message!" email and log back in to see who's been trying to reach them; odds are high that any such emails are either ignored, sent to the spam folder or deleted without being read in the first place.

You may also want to watch out for active profiles by people who don't actually spend the money to subscribe. Some dating sites will let you post your profile for free, but have to pay extra to actually send messages. These sorts of accounts will have unsubtle clues as to how to reach them elsewhere… and 9 times out of 10, they're spammers anyway. Don't waste your time.

---

[1] And *that* was one of the more restrained suggestions…

[2] Metaphorically *or* literally.

[3] Don't.

NINE

LEARNING TO MONEYBALL OKCUPID

LOVE AND MATH - A MATCH.COM MADE IN HEAVEN

One of the more popular news stories of 2014 was the story of how Chris McKinlay, a mathematics PhD candidate, "hacked" OKCupid in order to find love. Naturally, this inspired both wonder – OMG, nerds can break the code and get laid! – and a surprising amount of misdirected anger from people who seemed to believe that McKinlay was doing something fiendish and underhanded, a digital pick-up artist who dehumanized women by trying to reduce seduction into numbers and becoming an online Svengali.

The truth however, was much more prosaic.

McKinlay did what many nerds have done before: he attempted to solve a problem by taking his strengths – research, coding and statistical sampling – and applying them to the task at hand. Rather than finding some ruthless exploit in the human psyche that was somehow vulnerable to math or injecting foreign code into the site's database, McKinlay simply managed to moneyball OKCupid. Much as Billy Beane decided to apply math and statistical analysis to baseball - or, for that matter, how Chris Coyne, Christian Rudder, Sam Yagan, and Max Krohn applied data analysis to compatibility - McKinlay compiled data and used OkCupid's analytical system to make him appear more often in people's searches.

Part of OKCupid's appeal is its match algorithm that promises to help you find your ideal match - "provided you're honest", according to the developers. From the user's side of things, it's fairly simple. You answer a series of questions that supposedly tell the system who you are and what you're looking for in a match. With each question, you follow the same procedure: you answer the question for yourself, you select the answer that your ideal match would provide and then decide how important the question is to you. Your answer and its importance are given a numeric value, which allows them to be calculated against your match's answers. This, in turn, gives you the match percentage.

In OKCupid, your compatibility score directly affects the visibility of your profile to other people. The lower your compatibility with an individual, the less likely you were to show up in their searches. But because most people pay little to no attention to how the matching system works, they don't recognize how the way they answer the questions affects who appears in their searches. By answering willy-nilly, they inadvertently affect their compatibility with other people. Many questions have nothing to do with personality or relationships at all. Questions such as "If you turn a left-handed glove inside out, which hand does it fit on?" are cute logic puzzles but have nothing to do with actual compatibility. Answering the question "wrong"[1] can tank your compatibility with potential matches.

By paying attention and answering questions strategically, you can have much greater control over your match percentages. Not only will this help maximize your visibility in other people's searches, but a higher match percentage means that people will be more likely to respond to you… or even to reach out to *you*, first. OKCupid performed a number of sociological experiments with their user base. In one instance, they informed people with poor match scores - 30% or less - that they were actually a *higher* match percentage. When the site displayed a 90% match, the odds of someone exchanging a first message increased significantly. Just as importantly, though, after having sent *one* message, the odds of the pair exchanging *four* messages - that is, an exchange of messages becoming a conversation - increased as well.

This should tell you the importance of managing your questions and optimizing your match percentages and why McKinlay's findings can be important to you. You *want* as many matches at 90% or better as you can arrange. You don't need to be a coding wiz and use python scripts and data miners to collate questions in order to maximize your profile's visibility. You just need to understand how to make the system work in your favor.

And to do that, you need to take a look at what goes on under the hood at OKCupid.

UNDERSTAND THE SYSTEM TO WORK THE SYSTEM

If you want to maximize your profile's visibility, then you have to understand how the system works. Let's get into the meat of how OKCupid calculates the value of your questions - all helpfully provided by OKCupid themselves.[2]

Each question you answer requires that you mark how important it is to you. You have three choices[3]:

1. A little important
2. Somewhat important
3. Very Important

Each of these answers has a numeric value. "A little important" is 1 point, "somewhat important" is 10 points and "very important" is worth 50 points. If you choose "all of the above" on any of the questions, it's listed as "irrelevant" and given 0 points. The algorithm calculates the value of every question you answered and takes the sum as your maximum value - so if you answered 5 questions and weighted each of them as "somewhat important" at 10 points each, your maximum value would be 50 points. It then compares the questions that you and your match both answered; each question that your match answers the way that you hoped they would awards them points based on the importance of that question. So, taking our example again: if they answered only one question "correctly", they would have 10 points out of 50 or only

20% satisfaction.

Similarly, your questions are ranked against *their* answers. To make the math easier, we'll assume that they also only answered 5 questions, but ranked them all as "very important" - which means they're worth 50 points each - giving them a maximum satisfaction value of 250. You answered three out of the five correctly, giving you 150 points out of 250 or 60% satisfaction.

Your match percentage is calculated by multiplying the satisfaction and taking the square root of the answer. So in this case, you and this random person would only be approximately 35% compatible - not very compatible at all.

The other factor that affects your match percentage is the number of questions answered. OKCupid adjusts your match percentage by a margin of error based on the number of questions you've answered in common. In the case of this example, you have 5 mutually answered questions. OkCupid gives this a margin of error of 20% - so your displayed compatibility percentage would be 15%. This, frankly, sucks. But then, even if you'd answered every question the same way, your maximum compatibility score would be 80%. Not a bad score, all things considered…

but it means that you're not going to show up terribly high in anybody's searches. In online dating sites, positioning is everything. Much as with Google search results, you want to show up on the first page at the very least, and as close to the top of the results page as you can. You want to minimize the margin of error, so that you can have as high a match percentage as possible. To get there, you need to answer more questions; the more mutually answered questions you have, the lower the margin of error.

At the same time however, you want don't want to spend all of your time going through answering thousands upon thousands of questions. Not only is it a waste of time, but it offers you no material benefit. You hit severely diminishing returns past 100 questions (which gives you a maximum match of 99%) and the advantages bottom out entirely at 500 questions (with a maximum match of 99.8%) The .1% difference between 500 questions and 1000 questions is statistically insignificant enough that it's simply not worth your time.

Answer The Right Questions

When most people sign up for OKCupid, they tend to answer the questions as the come, with little thought to questions of compatibility or relevance. They may check for specific answers under the "The Two of Us" tab, but they rarely put much thought into what they're answering and why.

You, on the other hand, want to put some serious thought into how you answer yours. Now that you understand more about how weighting the questions can affect who sees your profile, it's important to be strategic with the questions you choose to answer. Not every question is created equal. Asking which number comes next in a sequence may make for a fun brain teaser, but it has nothing to do with what you're looking for in a partner. It's just a potential loss of compatibility points. Similarly, some questions are more popular than others. Since your compatibility score is based on questions that you've *both* answered, there's a distinct advantage to focusing on questions that show up more often in peoples' profiles. The more popular questions you answer, the more opportunities to give points towards compatibility scores, which in turn increases the number of profiles you will encounter. A question that you *don't* share with your matches, on the other hand, doesn't count towards compatibility and has the net effect of *removing* people from your searches. If you're using McKinlay's strategy, answering 100 of the *right* questions is more beneficial than answering 1000 of the *wrong* ones

So with all of this in mind, you want to start with a clean slate. If you're building a new profile, you're set. If you already have a profile - or you started answering questions *before* you got to this chapter - then clear all your answers. You're going to start fresh from the beginning.

Next: you're going to start picking and choosing which questions to answer and which ones to skip.

Your strategy is going to be to find the balance between increasing your match percentage - by giving out points on popular or common questions - while making sure you're finding the people you want to be matched up with by answering questions strategically. You want to answer questions that are actually relevant to the sort of relationship you're looking for and the kind of person you want to meet. Any question that's not directly relevant to your relationship goals simply throws noise into your signal and makes it harder to find the *right* matches. If the question doesn't apply to you or doesn't have an answer that you feel is germane to your search, skip it.

As you go through, consider the potential answers and the effects that the weighting will have on your matches. You want to cast your net widely (but accurately), after all; part of the secret to McKinlay's success was simple: he gave certain questions greater statistical weight than others. Whenever there was a chance to give a potential match more points - increasing their compatibility score - he would weigh that question's importance accordingly. When the question had a greater chance to *lose* points, he would rate it as being "irrelevant" or skip it entirely. Using this strategy, you would want to rate questions with two or three acceptable answers as "very important"; because there are so many acceptable answers, you want to increase that question's statistical weight in order to maximize the opportunity. On the other hand, a question with a simple yes/no answer represents a chance to *lose* points - you have a 50/50 chance of your match answering "wrong" and so you'd want to minimize its influence on your overall score.

The only time that you would want to rate a binary question as "very important" is if the question is something that you feel *very* strongly about. In this case, you would *want* to lower your compatibility score with anyone who disagreed with you; you want to filter out people you're not a genuine match with.

The other thing to keep in mind: that compatibility algorithm works both ways; your matches can lower their score by answering your questions incorrectly but you can lower *your* score with *them* the same way. Be choosey about which questions you answer. Giving unacceptable answers can lower your compatibility. An unanswered question doesn't affect the score either way.

As you're going through and answering these questions, you'll want to occasionally check to see what questions your matches are answering. By choosing "The Two of Us" and checking the "What They Care About" and "Unanswered By You" options, you'll find questions that you may have missed that your matches care strongly about. Find a few questions that they've answered that are relevant to your dating life and answer those, then check other match's questions. As you do this, you'll notice some coming up with greater regularity. These are questions you will want to pay special attention to, especially ones that apply to what you're looking for.

Once you've reached that sweet spot between 100 and 500 questions, you'll notice that the number of people who show up in your searches will have changed. If you've been careful, you'll find that you have drastically increased the number of high-quality matches. In fact, you should be getting more visitors to your profile than you've had before. That high compatibility number is a compelling draw. It won't do the work *for* you but it'll certainly entice more people to check you out.

Now with that having been said: there's answering questions strategically and then there's trying to game the system. Regardless of what you're looking for, trying to figure out what your dream match wants and answering questions accordingly is a mistake. Even if all you're looking for is a no-strings one night stand, lying or misrepresenting yourself works against you. Answering questions dishonestly makes it harder to match with people you're *actually* compatible with. By lying or creating a false persona, you're actually making it *harder* on yourself to find the people you're looking for, will only increase the number of false positives, dead-end conversations and shitty first dates. By trying to give people what you think they want to hear, versus who you actually are, you're making more work for yourself - something you don't need. The data backs this up as well: a pair of users with a *genuinely* higher match percentage is more likely to start a conversation than someone who simply tried to play the odds, regardless of his true answers.

Besides: people aren't stupid. Your matches will figure out pretty quickly that something's up when the way that you answered your questions doesn't line up with either your profile or the way you talk or behave around them. To quote Mark Twain: "If you tell the truth, you don't have to remember what you said."

GET NOTICED

Part of optimizing your time on OkCupid means being an active user. Remember when I mentioned the zombie profile - those profiles that are still live but abandoned? Part of how OkCupid de-emphasizes zombie profiles is by rewarding users who log in regularly while downplaying users that don't. More active users show up higher in searches and on the front page, which can help drive users to their pages. This is important because another key component to making OkCupid work in your favor is to make sure that people notice you. After all, it doesn't do you any good to have an incredible match percentage if they don't know you're there. There are plenty of people who don't go searching for profiles, or who may have settings that filter people out unknowingly.

You don't want that. You've spent all this time working on your profile and you want to show it off a little! So you want to make sure that you raise your visibility by using the tools the site gives you while continuing to improve your profile over time.

First of all: tweak your profile regularly. Writing a dating profile isn't a one-and-done scenario. You're always changing and growing as a person and your profile should reflect this. You'll think of better ways to phrase things, more efficient ways of getting your point across and keywords that you want to include in your profile. Changing things up raises your activity level on the site, and those edits show up on the front page.

You should also add photos of yourself. New photos are especially eye-catching and can prompt people who may have ignored you before to check you out... and for people to check you out a second time, for that matter. Swapping your primary photo can result in your bringing new eyeballs to your page.

Timing and traffic count for visibility as well; making changes during peak traffic periods means that more users will be around to see the changes you've made crop up on the front page. Fortunately, OkCupid will let you know when traffic is high - the "boost profile" button will glow like a sexed up neon firefly, begging you to spend money.

Another part of getting people's attention and drawing them to your profile is very simple: visit them first.

This was another interesting discovery from

McKinlay's experiments: by visiting his match's profiles, he could prompt them to visit *his* in return. In fact, it became one of the most successful ways to get women to contact *him* first. He wrote a Python script to systematically visit every profile within his parameters that had a high match percentage, sorted by age; it would start at the oldest potential matches and work its way through all of them at 41 years old before resetting and then going through everyone who was 40 years old. As a result: he was showing up in the visitor logs of hundreds to thousands of women. Out of those, a significant percentage would be intrigued enough to click through and visit his carefully optimized profile. This approach gave him a better rate of return on effort than he was getting by cold-contacting women.

Of course, you may not be a coder or have the time to create and fine-tune scripts to nudge your potential matches, and most dating sites actively look for and disable bots anyway. But while you may not be able to replicate the speed and efficiency of a 'bot, you can help make sure you're getting noticed by investing some time in your searches. Start by browsing profiles, with the filter set to "Best match" then click through each match, one after another. Don't worry about reading their profiles; you're just wanting to show up in their visitor's log. Your photo should entice their curiosity while your profile and carefully managed match percentage will draw them in.

ONLINE IS ONLY HALF THE BATTLE

It's important to remember: the key to online dating is *dating*. Maximizing your compatibility score and getting more visitors and more messages is great... but optimizing your profile just gets people's attention. No matter how much people may love your profile or your photos, no matter how much chemistry you may have online, you *still* need to be able to wow them in person. One of the key points in McKinlay's story is that he while he went on over 50 first dates, he had *far* fewer second or third ones before meeting his girlfriend.

This, ultimately, is a part of dating, no matter how you meet them; there are going to be people that you just don't work with for one reason or another, and no amount of talking on IM or Skype or on the phone is going to let you know in advance. If you want things to work, you're going to have to put in the effort to have an amazing first date and see where it goes.

---

[1] Especially if you're the sort of smart-ass who tries to explain why the question's premise is flawed

² https://www.okcupid.com/help/match-percentages if you want to check it out for yourself.

³ Technical note: OKCupid's help page about the match percentages lists five choices, but the questions themselves offer three - a relatively recent change. The help page has yet to be updated to reflect the new choices.

I've contacted OkCupid about how this changes answers' mathematical weighting, but at the time of this writing, I haven't heard back. That being said: this doesn't materially affect the way that you'll want to answer questions.

TEN

FREQUENTLY ASKED QUESTIONS

WHAT'S THE ETTIQUETTE ON CHECKING YOUR DATE'S ONLINE PROFILE?

One of the more frustrating aspects of dating culture is that technology frequently outpaces our ability to develop new rules of etiquette and best behavior. This is never more noticeable than when it comes to our digital lives. Between Google, Facebook, Twitter, Instagram and, of course, online dating sites, we have more ways of communicating with (and investigating) our dates than ever before. Ann Landers could never have anticipated the myriad questions of social etiquette that come with a life lived primarily online.

Among the more perplexing questions is: what are the rules when it comes to interacting with a match online, before you're in a relationship? Is it OK to track them down on Facebook before you've met? What about following them on Twitter? Is Googling them an invasion of privacy or simply a way of doing your due diligence before you meet? And how do you handle things when you can *see* that your date is still active on Match and OkCupid?

Well, never let it be said that I'm averse to cutting the Gordian knot of social media and social rules.

When Should You Friend Them On Facebook?

Facebook is, in many ways, a walled garden. It may be an especially *large* one, with hundreds or even thousands of people allowed access... but it's still considered to be a "private" space. Tracking down a date before you've gotten explicit permission to send her a friend request could be seen as being overly eager and displaying low social intelligence at best. Plus, considering the issues that Facebook has had with quietly changing people's privacy settings, it could feel like a significant violation. Do yourself a favor: ask if you can send them a friend request before you go trying to find them. And wait until you've had a couple solid dates before you ask.

What About Following Them On Twitter?

Twitter, on the other hand is less of a private garden and somewhere between a conversation in a crowded bar and standing on a soapbox on a street corner. There's less of of a general expectation of privacy by design, but that doesn't necessarily make it a free-for-all. Jumping into somebody's mentions without a connection to them can be akin to barging into a conversation between friends. Following a person on Twitter is less personal, but it's still probably a good idea to hold off at first.

What About Googling?

One of the polite fictions of modern society is that we don't Google our friends and dates. Everybody *does*, of course - these days it's practically part of the courtship process - but it's not polite to acknowledge it openly. That having been said, unless you discover that your date has a criminal record, a history of dangerous behavior or just plain doesn't *exist*[1], don't mention it. And while you're at it: don't dig too deeply and do *not* bring up anything you've learned about them. I've had friends whose dates started bringing up *incredibly* personal information about my friends' families that said dates had dug up on Google. It's intensely disturbing and stalker-y and will kill the attraction deader than disco.

What About Checking On Their Dating Profiles?

This is where things get interesting. When you're dating someone you've met in person, it's easier to pretend that that they're not seeing anyone else; after all, it's the rare person who's so rude as to flirt with someone else right in front of you while on a date. When you meet someone on an online dating site, on the other hand, it's not hard to "accidentally" notice that UCLAGal84 has been logging into her account even after you've gone on a few dates. Likewise, it's also difficult to not feel at least a *little* stung over the idea that they're still (potentially) flirting with other people. Sure, intellectually you know you're not exclusive and it's far too early to even *think* about it. But still… it stings.

Of course, the big question is: *are* they flirting with other people? People log into their profiles for a number of reasons: to clear out old messages, to read messages from people who've written to them and say "no thanks", to continue conversations with people they were talking with before. Many sites have active forums and blogs as well as matchmaking services. OkCupid spent years positioning itself as as social network as well as a dating site. And yes, they may well be logging in to search for or flirt with other people. Is it *likely* that they're on there for reasons other than to meet other people? To be honest: no. Probably not. But the fact of the matter is: you don't *know*. All you're doing is needlessly increasing your anxiety over this person, a person who, let us be frank, you barely know.

I completely understand the impulse to check and the anxious fear that they might decide to ditch you for this other person they're meeting. However, constantly checking their profile (and showing up repeatedly in their visitor's logs) isn't going to *prevent* them from seeing other people.

And to be perfectly frank, if they *do* decide to explore things with somebody else, it's just an indicator that you two weren't all that compatible in the first place and it wouldn't have worked out *anyway*.

Besides: just because they're talking to - or even going out with - someone else, it doesn't mean that they're *not* going to decide they'd rather pursue a relationship with *you*. For all you know, that flirtation or date could be the moment that makes them realize how much they like you.

Until you've both agreed to disable your profiles, it's best to simply pretend that you can't see theirs. Out of sight, out of mind.

What Do You Do When Nobody Visits Your Profile?

There's something especially humiliating when you realize that your profile isn't attracting *any* traffic whatsoever. That empty "recent visitors" entry seems to mock you, a confirmation of every fear and insecurity you've ever had and a sign that you're simply doomed to be alone forever.

But before you decide that you're a social pariah, take some time to do some revisions.

The first thing you need to do is get some new photos. Photos are the first line of interest when it comes to dating profiles; if nobody is visiting your profile, then the odds are that your primary photo is simply not eye-catching enough. It may be awkwardly cropped, making it look like you're trying to hide an ex. You may not be visible in the thumbnail. You may have more than one person in the photo, leaving people confused as to which one is you. Or it simply may be a bad photo. As I said earlier, the best primary photo is a clear shot of your head and shoulders. Your potential matches want to know what you look like! Don't make it harder for them; the more they have to work, the less likely they are to click through. You may want to consider having some photos taken by a professional; they can help ensure you have a sharp looking profile photo.

Next, check your vital statistics. There may be a setting or two in there that is causing you to not show up in people's searches. Most people filter for age, gender, height, build, and location at the bare minimum. Leaving out any of that information guarantees that you won't show up in their searches.

Following that, refer back to chapter 8 and check to make sure you're not making any of those mistakes. Revising your profile is a good idea in general, but if you're getting next to no (or any) visitors and responses, then something in there is likely turning them off. If you're on OkCupid, consider ditching your questions and starting over to help increase potential compatibility scores.

If all of this *still* doesn't work, then it's time to start doing some A/B testing to try to narrow in on the problem. Start by adjusting your details, one at a time. Give yourself an extra inch or two (but not three) in height or shave a couple years off your age. Set your build to "average". This is the one time I'm giving you permission to fudge the truth a little; this is being done in the name of science. Give yourself a couple of days with each new setting and see whether that affects your response rate before changing it back and testing the next setting. If you're in an open relationship, you may want to consider setting your relationship status to "single" in order to appear in people's searches. This is one of the few times I consider it ok to be a tad dishonest; even people who are open to dating people in open relationships tend to search for "single" rather than "everyone". It is vital, however, that you make your relationship status clear in your profile and in your messages; people have a right to make an informed decision about whether or not they want to message or meet you.

Another thing to consider: look at who you're messaging. How compatible are you *really*? Are you aiming strictly at people for their looks, rather than what you have in common? Are you messaging people who don't live within a reasonable distance? Note: reasonable is going to vary depending on your location. In Manhattan, an unreasonable distance is frequently someone who lives in one of the outer boroughs or New Jersey. In parts of Ohio, it may be within a certain commute's length. As a general rule of thumb, if it would take you more than 45 minutes to reach them by car, odds are good they're not going to be interested in dating you. Travel time *is* a factor; having to plan an extra hour and a half to two hours on the road for a date is enough to dissuade a lot of people.

While normally I advise against it, if you're not getting many (or *any*) visitors, you may also want to consider paying for a little extra visibility. OKCupid has it's Boost feature that ensures more people will see your profile, while Match, Zoosk and other sites have pay-for-exposure options that highlight your profile and make you stand out more. This can also be a way of testing changes you've made to your profile - that extra prominence can net you more potential reactions to your improvements.

Finally: consider the site. You, for whatever reason, may be a poor fit - whether it be demographic, personality type or lifestyle - for the site you're on. Some people do better on Match than they do on OkCupid or Plenty of Fish. Others do better on Christian Mingle or Coffee Meets Bagel. It can take some trial and error to find the right place - and the right profile - for you.

SHE DIDN'T WRITE BACK. WHAT DO I DO NOW?

A lot of people want to know what they should do

when they don't get a response from someone they've messaged. More often than not, they want to know if there's some way to prompt the other person to reply and give them a shot.

The thing is: no reply *is* a reply. It's "I'm not interested."

If they're not into what you have to offer, there's no amount of nudging that's going to change their mind; at best, you're going to continue to be ignored. At worst, you're going to get blocked and reported. Nobody has ever been successfully nagged into liking somebody else. Similarly, no woman has ever been successfully convinced that maybe she was wrong for rejecting someone by the argument of "Fuck you bitch, you're ugly."

If you're wondering why women are more likely to ignore a message instead of saying "Thanks, but no thanks", you can thank the assholes who yell at her for turning them down.

Every introductory message you send on a dating site should be fired and forgotten. Don't try to read the tea leaves over how long it's taken them to get back to you or not; not everybody is on your schedule. Either they'll be interested enough to respond, or they won't. Getting caught up on whether this person or that person has responded or not does nothing but cause you grief for no good reason. This is why read receipts are a bad idea; knowing that someone read your message and hasn't responded is only going to make you wonder what you might have done wrong. Message them once and move on to the next person. If you hear back from them, *great*. If not, no biggie, time to message someone else.

And just FYI: if they *were* going to respond to you but hadn't yet, poking them about it is a good way to change their minds.

WHAT DO YOU DO IF SHE DOESN'T LOOK LIKE HER PHOTOS

Straight talk: there're fakers out there. Many people - men and women both - will play fast and loose with the truth; they may shave a few years off their age, add a few inches to their height or downplay their build. This, frankly, is so common that it's to be expected. The other thing - the bigger lie - that they'll do is use deceptive photos. Sometimes it's as simple as being an out of date picture. Other times they may have done a little digital cosmetic surgery; the camera may add ten pounds but Photoshop can take off twenty.

Now let's be clear: when given the opportunity, people will make sure to show off their best side - they'll pose a way they know shows themselves off to their best advantage. Makeup, hair styles, flattering light... we *all* take the opportunities to make ourselves look our best. That's an accepted part of online dating. I've yet to see a single dating profile with nothing but photos of themselves when they've just rolled right out of bed.

It's when people look *significantly* different that it becomes an issue.

So what do you do? Well, you need to ask yourself an honest question: how much does this difference matter to you? Yes physical attraction is important to a relationship... but is the difference between the picture and reality so dramatically different that you couldn't possibly be interested in them now? Are looks the *only* reason that you were planning on meeting them or were you interested in their personality too?

If you're *so* traumatized by the apparent deception, you could always just bail without saying another word. But to be perfectly honest, I find this to be a coward's way out. This is one of the benefits of the pre-date date; unless they are *so* very different that it's literally impossible for them to have been the person in the photo, it's hardly the end of the world to have a cup of coffee and then take off after a half-hour. In a worst case scenario: you're out 30 minutes and three bucks for coffee. In a best case scenario, you may find that there's something about them you like anyway.

But honestly: once you've spent some time going through profiles and meeting people, you'll start getting the hang of averaging out what people look like based on the sum of their photos and telling who's trying to hide what and how. The number of out and out liars is small enough that if you meet more than one then you're having an especially bad streak of luck.

HOW DO I SPOT A FAKE PROFILE?

One of the risks people worry about when it comes to online dating is running into a faker. A liar. A scammer. A catfish.² It's the longest running joke about online dating - that 21 year old cheerleader is actually a 56 year old man in disguise - but it *does* happen on occasion. Sometimes it's a person playing a trick on you. Sometimes they're trolling you. Sometimes they're running a con; many people will use an online identity in order to scam money from lonely men and women. In 2012, Notre Dame football star Manti Te'o was famously tricked into believing he was in a relationship with a woman who didn't actually exist.

Spotting a faked identity is equal parts instinct and research. Some fakers are of the painfully obvious "Hello, I am $RICH_PERSON from Nigeria and I want to employ you, random Internet person, in my money-laundering scheme" style; the scammers behind these are going trawling for suckers and only want the most gullible. Others will have put considerably more time and effort into their fake identities and making them seem "real." None of these tips are going to be 100% effective in ferreting out a fake profile – some fakes are extremely good – but in combination, these will help keep you from being gulled.

Are They Too Good To Be True?

This can be the hard one because we desperately want to believe that the Danish supermodel with the incredible rack who also happens to love 3rd Ed. D&D and Tennant-era Doctor Who thinks we're sexy and wants to date us. We all want to believe that someone so amazing could fall in love with our minds and hearts long before they encounter the too, too flawed flesh that we inhabit. And while that can and does happen… well, to be perfectly honest, it ain't worth betting the house (or your heart) on.

Catfish prey on the fact that we all believe we're special and that our beauty may well lie deep within rather than on the surface and the hope that someday somebody incredible will see that. They go out of their way to embody that fantasy; they create an illusion so compelling that you become complicit in your own defrauding because you desperately want it to be true.

You have to be honest with yourself: why would this person suddenly fall for you so quickly – and catfish tend to move very fast. Is it possible that this is too convenient, too perfect? If so, you owe it to yourself to check. If it's real, then your Internet sweetie should have no problem with your investigating; presumably they have nothing to hide.

If they get offended and indignant that you don't trust them, then it should be a warning to you that something may not be as it seems.

Are They Refusing To Meet You In Person?

As I've said before: while some people will prefer to take more time than others to meet, the point of an online dating site is to meet *off*line. Someone who continually refuses to meet in person is sending you a message. Once is happenstance. Twice is coincidence. Three times is reason to be suspicious. If they're continually having last minute conflicts that mean they have to cancel, incredibly busy schedules that just show no sign of ever letting up or taking longer to decide that they trust you than you're willing to wait, then something's up. Maybe they're just not interested… or maybe they're not who they're presenting themselves as.

If you've been trading pictures and sexting back and forth, but they won't meet you in person, then you should be *very* suspicious and ready to end things.

Google Them

As more and more of our lives are lived online, it's increasingly difficult to not leave traceable footprints behind. A slim Google profile may not mean much – many of my childhood friends don't have much presence if you just search their names – but many of the provided details of their lives should be easily found. Some high-schools and colleges have publicly searchable alumni lists and even yearbooks. If they have an especially notable or unusual career – many a young man has had his heart broken by a supposed "model" – it should be easy to find information about them online. If not the individual specifically then their employer, organizations that they may belong to, etc. Remember while you're searching to cross-reference the information you're finding with the information they've provided you, especially if they have a common name. Deborah Lee from Anchorage, Alaska is not likely to be the same Deborah Lee from Manassas, Virginia.

Check Their Social Media Presence

In this day and age, the number of people who don't have a presence on social networks are vanishingly small – and the younger they are, the more likely they are to have an extensive one. If you harbor suspicions, start to examine their online accounts. Does he or she have a Facebook page? If so, how many friends do they have? How many posts and photos have they been tagged in? What have they liked, what timelines have they written on? Not being wildly active or having few Facebook friends is not damning evidence by any stretch – not everybody is a digital social butterfly after all – but it can be a cause for suspicion, especially if their friends are predominantly single members of their preferred gender.

Similarly, check their Twitter feed – who do they follow, who follows them, how many people do they converse with and how many hashtags and trending topics do they take part in?

Yes, I said earlier that tracking people down on Facebook is stalker-y behavior. This is the exception. By this point, your Spidey-sense has probably been tingling for a while and you're trying to confirm they are who they *say* they are.

Google Image Search Is Your New Best Friend

Most catfish rely on stolen photos for their profiles. Many will scour popular sites like DeviantArt or ModelMayhem to find attractive stand-ins, while some – notably Foreign Bride brokers – will use photos of known porn-stars. Others will steal photos from unlocked Facebook and Instagram accounts – as was the case of "Lennay Kekua", Manti Te'o's fake girlfriend – in order to create a more authentic feel.

Using these photos, however, is often their greatest Achilles' heel; because these photos came from other websites, it's possible to trace them back to their origin. Google now allows for reverse image searches – simply drag a .jpg or .gif to the search bar and you can track down where else those photos appear online. Firefox, Opera and Chrome all have extensions that make reverse image searching a simple click away in your browser.

This isn't foolproof: some scammers will use a third party as an (sometimes unwitting) accomplice for custom photos that don't appear anywhere else online. But if you suspect a catfish situation, Google's Reverse Image Search should be the first thing you check.

Skype Is Your Next Best Friend

Some catfish will refuse to talk on the phone, preferring to text. Others have no problem speaking on the phone…. but this ultimately proves nothing. If you suspect a catfish, you need to get them on camera.

We are now at the point where it is entirely reasonable to expect that most of the people we interact with online have access to a webcam and video-conferencing software. Skype is the most obvious (and free!) example, but Adium, Message, Trillian, Meebo, G-chat and Yahoo all offer video chatting as well as instant messaging. Tiny Chat, StickCam and Google+ Hangouts also allow video conferencing. Even our smartphones also have video chat capabilities now; the iPhone has FaceTime and Skype while Android phones have Skype, Fring and Google Talk.

So frankly, if your Internet sweetie can't or won't Skype with you, it's a cause for potential concern.

If you're especially un-trusting, you can always call or IM them (or arrange for a friend to do so, off cam) in the middle of your cam session.

Beware of the Drama Bomb

One of the most frequent signs of a catfish is a high drama quotient. Many fake profiles and identities are rife with histrionics and melodramatic goings on – family members who come down with dramatic diseases or even die, spectacular accidents, conveniently timed job losses, fights with dear friends, vengeful exes – in order to better take advantage of their audience's compassion and encourage White Knight-ery. These splashy incidents also serve as convenient distractions to divert suspicion. Are you starting to ask probing questions? Time to kill off grandma! Now you're an insensitive cad for daring to interrogate her during her time of need.

He who lives by the drama however, dies by the drama. Google once again is your friend; major incidents such as traffic accidents, muggings, assaults and even deaths get documented and logged online. Newspaper crime blotters, incident reports and obituaries are all searchable now and easily found with some basic Google-Fu.

If someone in your life is having constant issues in his or her life – especially if they occur at opportune moments, keeping them from meeting you in person or distracting you from a fight – it's time to be suspicious. Once is happenstance. Twice is coincidence. Three times is somebody bullshitting you. Your mantra should always be trust… but verify.

---

[1] AKA: Catfishing. More on that in a moment.

[2] A catfish is someone who creates a fake online persona via social media in order to fool others, especially for the pursuit of an online relationship. Named for the popular documentary by Ariel and Nev Shulmann.

ELEVEN

THE MOST IMPORTANT ADVICE I CAN OFFER

DATING SHOULD BE FUN

One of the things that will always be true about dating is simple: there are no quick fixes and easy answers. Dating is a skill and that skill takes time and practice to improve, and that includes online dating. You may need to take more than one pass on your dating profile as you develop your voice and presence online. You may have to experiment with different photos, different approaches to messaging people, even different dating sites as you find what works for you.

However, none of this matters if you're not enjoying yourself. Dating should be *fun*. Some parts of it may not be as diverting as others, but the overall process should be enjoyable. Even if you're looking for someone to settle down with, you should be able to take pleasure from the process, whether the excitement of meeting somebody new or the thrill of discovery as you get to know people better. Even little things like getting more visitors as you fine-tune your profile can be a source of encouragement. In many ways it can be like a game, finding the best path towards your ultimate goal.

That's why the best advice I can give you is that if you're not enjoying yourself, then take some time off and give yourself a break.

Fun is an important part of attraction after all, and if you're not having fun, people will respond to that. If clicking through profile after profile drains the life out of you and the idea of sending one more message is like sandpaper to your soul, then it's going to affect *every* aspect of your dating life. That sense of dread and unhappiness will come through in every message you send and every line you write and make things that much harder than it should be.

Suspend your account for a little while and take some time for yourself. Pursue your interests, develop some new hobbies, do the things that breathe new life into your tired body and recharge your soul. Come back when you're rested, relaxed and ready to give the ol' town a wedgie again. That feeling of renewal may be just what you need to make online dating fun again.

I won't lie: dating can be frustrating, even maddening at times. There will be false positives. There will be people with whom you simply aren't compatible or who just aren't interested in you.

But then you'll find the ones who *are*. The ones who get you, and that hit all the right notes for you too. And when you meet those awesome people and you have that moment when it all *clicks?*

It will make everything *worth* it.

Good luck.

About The Author

Harris O'Malley (AKA Dr. NerdLove) is an Austin-based, internationally recognized blogger and dating coach who provides geek dating advice at Paging Dr. NerdLove and his bi-weekly advice column "Ask Dr. NerdLove" on Kotaku.

O'Malley been featured in The Guardian, The Washington Post, The Austin-American Statesman, New York Magazine Think Progress, Lifehacker, Wired, Buzzfeed, Huffington Post Live, Sex Nerd Sandra, The Art of Charm, Sex With Timaree, Daily Life, Slate, MTV's Guy Code, Boing Boing and The Harvard Business Journal. He has been named one of the top 10 geek dating blogs by DatingAdvice.com.

For more more advice on dating, sex & relationships, visit him online at www.doctornerdlove.com

Keep up with the latest from Dr. NerdLove:
twitter.com/DrNerdLove
facebook.com/DrNerdLove
doc@doctornerdlove.com

Printed in Germany
by Amazon Distribution
GmbH, Leipzig